'Jeremy is a true entrepreneur. In his writings he shares his journey and we learn how he has always believed that life is what we make of it, never the victim, never seeking to be the hero, Jeremy has just been determined to be independently wealthy and rely on no one else. Is it possible to teach entrepreneurship? I believe it is with the right role models and realism of what it takes. This book takes the reader through that real, scary, joyful and ultimately rewarding journey into wealth.'

Penny P   Youth
Academy

GO DO!

For People Who Have Always Wanted to Start a Business

Jeremy Harbour

CAPSTONE

Library of Congress Cataloging-in-Publication Data
Harbour, Jeremy.
   Go do! : for people who have always wanted to start a business / Jeremy Harbour.
   p. cm.
   ISBN 978-0-85708-274-9 (pbk.)
1. New business enterprises–Management.   2. Entrepreneurship.   I. Title.
   HD62.5.H369 2012
   658.1'1–dc23
                                   2012001819

A catalogue record for this book is available from the British Library.

ISBN 978-0-85708-274-9 (pbk) ISBN 978-0-857-08314-2 (ebk)
ISBN 978-0-857-08317-3 (ebk) ISBN 978-0-857-08316-6 (ebk)

Set in 11.5 on 15 pt Adobe Caslon Pro-Regular by Toppan Best-set Premedia
Limited
Printed in Great Britain by TJ International Ltd, Padstow, Cornwall, UK

CONTENTS

ACKNOWLEDGEMENTS

Thank you for buying my book. I heard that when Donald Trump's book was published he got sued for lots of money, so, for the avoidance of doubt, I've made it all up. I, therefore, can't accept any responsibility for anything negative that happens after listening to my advice. Of course if you go on to be hugely successful then I will humbly accept all the credit.

Sometimes life teaches you a lesson – I have learnt my fair share. If you don't get back up after being knocked down, then you didn't learn the lesson. I hope this book will give you a short cut past some of the painful lessons – but be ready to learn some of your own.

So many people have shaped my life it would be impossible to mention them all, but the real stars in my story are my family, in particular my Mum and Dad, Valerie and John Harbour. Without their support, advice and education over the years nothing would have been possible. Both of my grandmothers, Mabel (alive and kicking at 94 years old) and Freda (RIP), and my brother Ben have also helped me enormously on this journey. They say you can't choose your family, well, if I could I would choose this one.

Thank you.

INTRODUCTION

Warren Buffet was once asked how he could remember so much detail about thousands of stocks. His answer was 'Well, you start at A . . .'.

Every journey starts with a single step. The question is when will you take yours?

So, your financial advisor tells you to put half your salary into a pension scheme, which you won't see until you're almost dead, in order to make sure you will not have to sell your home to pay for your upkeep in a nursing home . . . bloomin' marvellous!

What about the guy who just went past in the Aston Martin, or the guy on the yacht in Monaco Harbour? Are they just lucky? Did they inherit it? Are they smarter than you? Probably not.

When you look at the richest people in the world nowadays, in either *Forbes* or the *Sunday Times* rich list, you will see that the list is almost entirely dominated by non-inherited wealth; a very different story to that of 20 years ago. When I was growing up the richest man in the world was the Sultan of Brunei, who owed his fortune to a combination of inherited and massive oil wealth. Today, the top three richest people are a telecoms guy in Mexico, a computer guy and a stocks and shares guy. They all started from zero. They all started with a single step. They all started at A.

Not only among the very top few, but all the way through the sprawling middle classes, the same thing is apparent. The transfer of wealth from what Warren Buffet calls 'the lucky sperm club', the world of inherited wealth, to the new world meritocracy, or earned wealth, is truly striking. This transfer of wealth and power represents a massive evolution of opportunity.

So how do you get your fair share?

There are many people who have made their wealth through a staggering variety of sources, through art, music, divorce or winning the lottery, but by far and away the greatest wealth creator is business – entrepreneurship in all its colours and forms. If you are starting from zero and you want to create a great life, have fun and just maybe become wealthy, then entrepreneurship wins hands down. You may think the odds of winning the lottery are reasonable. They're not. Most winners in life have to go out and do it for themselves.

What makes these entrepreneurs successful? To a great extent it is their self-belief that they can go and set up their own businesses and become a success. This self-belief isn't innate; it needs to be nurtured and encouraged, and it must survive in the face of much doubt. Society in general does not encourage this sort of behaviour; it tries to convince you that you need a job. This is passively drummed into us all on television, at school, from our parents and in newspapers and magazines. A job trades time for money, and time is very much finite, so it is, unfortunately, very hard to win through employment. Those who *Go Do* find an alternative route through life, where success is suddenly in their own hands.

For me, entrepreneurship is not about money, it is about life, fulfilment, learning, evolution and being the best version of *YOU* that you can be. When people complain about work, they often lament the fact that they cannot afford to leave their job. That complaint is a tacit admission that they are doing something they don't want to do for money alone. I would argue that many people with jobs, on the corporate treadmill, far more so than entrepreneurs, are all about the money – they get no fulfilment or development, just (often meagre) financial reward. What a compromised existence. I can see why they are so quick to say entrepreneurs are all about greed and money. As the French say, *que s'acuse, j'acuse* – he who accuses me, I accuse!

I also think the fluidity and dynamism of business provides an amazing creative outlet. Humans need a means of artistic expression to really feel content with life, and what a great outlet starting and running your own business is. You are creating a living, breathing thing from nothing – something that will take on a life of its own, a totally fluid and ever-changing canvas, which, without your attention, will waste away. The problem solving, the daily variation in tasks, the highs and the lows are irreplaceable human experiences and cannot be pigeon holed as good or bad.

I wrote this book for the people who always talk about starting a business, taking their first step, but never get round to it. The procrastinators, kicking it into the long grass and saying 'one day I would love to run my own business'. I want them to just Go Do.

It is not designed just as a way to encourage people to start their business – anyone can do that with a bit of motivational know-how – but also as a way to dispel the myths around what you need to start. I want to paint a picture of how life changing the experience can be, to such an extent that you will feel embarrassed by not finally getting on and doing it.

Remember that knowledge and ambition are nothing without action. What differentiates success and failure, by my definition of those words, in taking those first steps?

Family and security are important things, which can't be underestimated, but none of us want to get into old age feeling mournful about a load of things we thought about doing. We owe ourselves something more than that – far better to go for it and have a rich tapestry of a life, full of adventure, and to know that you have been in the pursuit of happiness.

It is far better to regret things you did do than things you didn't.

People feel a fear of failing in business, but surely it is better to fail in business and then try again than to fail in life, with no reruns? Think of bouncing your grandchild on your knee and telling them about your life. Did you do the same job for 40 years, have four weeks' holiday a year and retire on a tiny pension; or did you grab life by the horns and give it a good shake, with a roller coaster of ups and downs, thrills and excitement, anecdotes and adventures? My definition of failure would be to have nothing to tell that grandchild.

Others have a more cautious view of success and failure, and that is their right. I acknowledge that my definition might not be for everyone, but I want to ask you to come with me on a journey and, by reading this book, consider an alternative view.

Business and enterprise not only enrich the lives of the people involved, but impact on society itself, through employment, economic growth and philanthropy. Warren Buffet and Bill Gates have already given tens of billions of dollars to charity, and have committed to raise $600 billion from the 400 richest people in the world.

Let's put that in perspective – $600,000,000,000. The entire overseas aid and development budget for the UK in 2011 is £7.8 billion, or $10 billion dollars. The UK has a very large aid budget in comparison to other countries and is sometimes domestically criticised for its generosity and the efficiency with which it distributes funds, but two entrepreneurs who built massive organisations are going to pump 60 times as much as one of the world's largest economies into solving problems like global poverty and disease in the third world. One could strongly argue that entrepreneurs will be very well equipped to really target that spending and get more bang for the buck than an average government can.

So entrepreneurship can literally change the world.

Without our entrepreneurs we would be lost – there would be no economy as we know it, product development and technology would be decades behind and not configured half so creatively as they are, and the problems of the future would look much more frightening without innovators to help find solutions. So we must really salute those who make the effort to make a difference, rather than plod through life as a passenger.

Don't assume for a moment that entrepreneurs like myself have got everything right, or that I am luckier or cleverer than you. We all learn by making mistakes, and the information you hold in your hands has taken me 20 years to distil. Hopefully this means I will be able to help you avoid some of the very expensive lessons I have encountered on my journey, ensuring that – even if you replace them with your own – you will definitely be one step ahead!

In my career I have shown that you do not need to go to university or have any capital to start a business. I certainly didn't have any money when I started. But I did have the drive and commitment to get started and, in this book, I'm going to show you why taking that first step and starting a business will be the best decision you'll ever take.

If, as a result of writing this book, I manage to get men and women to start their journeys for the benefit of the world, then I will have succeeded.

Life has a momentum, it has ruts. If you are not careful you can spend a long time in a rut, literally missing years of your life.

Please don't surrender to the momentum of mediocrity, and enjoy the book.

CHAPTER 1

So who am I and how did I get started? Well, entrepreneurship came as naturally to me as walking and talking; I had never really considered anything else.

I blame the parents. I was born into a household that valued independence, entrepreneurship and learning. I was born in England, in a tiny village in the north of the county of Dorset (Thomas Hardy wrote a lot about this area and it is sometimes referred to as Hardy country). Our house sat at the foot of Hambledon Hill in the beautiful Blackmore Vale and our nearest neighbour was my grandmother, down the road. As a kid you want to get out, escape, make your own way, but it's a truism that you only truly appreciate the beauty of your roots when you go back in later life. My father was a farmer and my mother ran a beauty salon, initially from home and later in a purpose-built salon. For my part I adored growing up on a farm – running around playing with power tools, setting fire to myself and eating all sorts of things that should not be eaten. I am sure that is why I have such a good immune system now.

The greatest thing I learned, looking back, was the independence of life – the fact you can pretty much do what you want and only you can fully judge yourself and your actions.

In a house where one or both parents work, it's too easy to conclude that the choices ahead of you are limited to working for a corporation or for the government, whether as a civil servant, in the armed forces or for the state. But I was encouraged to believe that if I wanted to be an artist or a businessman, or pretty much anything I wanted, I just had to choose. I felt that opportunity was always close by. With farming being so seasonal, my father was always dreaming and scheming. We would talk about business ideas over breakfast and I would help him launch these sideline exploits over the years.

Unfortunately, I didn't get pocket money, but I look back at this as a great lesson itself; rather than getting hand outs, I was offered the chance to work for my parents in either business for £1 an hour.

My parents gave me lots of encouragement. Noticing that old ladies liked tea, I launched an early venture selling tea bags to the members of my granny's sewing club. It was a market waiting to be exploited. My mum's regular visits to wholesalers to buy supplies for the salon gave me the opportunity to buy tea in bulk and break it down into smaller lots. There wasn't a great margin to the business but I did make a profit.

Aged 11, I started cutting down the flowers from the garden, putting them in jam jars and selling them outside the salon to ladies coming to have treatments. This time my parents were less encouraging; decimating the garden didn't endear the business to them, so I had to call a premature halt to proceedings. However, my big hit came at Christmas, when my dad put me in charge of another sideline of his. We had a small orchard where, a few years earlier, Dad had planted loads of Christmas trees. These had finally grown to full size, but with the farm taking up so much time, a 12-year-old Jeremy was put in charge. I was told to do whatever it took to sell as many as possible and I could keep half of the sale proceeds. So I placed an advert in the local paper, put a sign on the road and got selling; one price if they helped themselves, another if I had to saw it down and more again if they wanted it digging up. One great outlet was a local gypsy who bought ten at a time to sell door to door. My first indirect sales channel!

After a couple of weeks I had cleared £1600; a fortune for a 12 year old in the 1980s – and I think a surprise to my parents as well. The only slight annoyance was that a family decision was made to spend the money on a new TV and video that we could all share, so I never saw my half. Lesson learned? Get it in writing!

Life

Two major events, in hindsight, shaped me as a child.

Firstly, when I was aged about ten, my older brother Christopher died, suddenly and for no apparent reason. Nowadays they label it sudden adult death syndrome. I was taken to hospital and wired up to look for defects or arrhythmia, but nothing (that I know of . . . mum?) was found.

I seemed to go to a lot of funerals while I was growing up: both my grandfathers, a kid from school and my brother. My grandmother on my mum's side was one of 14 children, so there was a steady stream of great uncles slowly disappearing.

I never thought this strange. Death was part of life, and it was some time before I realised this was not the same for everyone. I have since met friends in their 30s who have not yet had anyone in their immediate family or circle of friends die. I think it may have given me a perspective on life being finite that made me appreciate that you get only one shot in this world – so make it count. Treat every day as your last and one day you will be right!

Secondly, my father's farming business failed. My parents were forced to sell the family home and we went from being an affluent, middle class, happy family to having our lives turned upside down and having to start again from scratch. In hindsight this was a great lesson in resilience, independence and how life throws curve balls every so often – so don't judge the ball, judge the way you handle it.

I do not have children so I do not yet completely understand how devastating it must have been for my parents to lose a son, but I have a pretty good idea.

Losing a business hurts too, though on nowhere near the same scale. I do know what it is like to have that happen, and whilst affording nothing like the grief that rises from a death, it can be a real emotional roller coaster. I do not envy my parents at all. However, the experience lit a fire in my belly to succeed that has burned strong since and has shaped my life. I had a taste of wealth at an age when it could not really be appreciated, but lost it as a teenager when I would have appreciated the benefits of what we had.

I am glad in a way that I did, as I learnt the value of making my own money and in experiencing the enjoyment of hatching a plan and making it work.

Shakespeare said: 'Far better to have loved and lost than never to have loved at all', and so I suppose I had developed a taste for it – and have strived ever since to get it back again.

'I did not make much money in this life, but I had great fun trying'

My grandmother, Freda Harbour, on her deathbed; the last thing she said to me.

School

School was okay but I didn't thrive. I was a bit dyslexic and frankly wasn't that interested; but I have a great memory so I learned a lot of stuff. If you want to know Boyle's law, Pythagoras' theorem or Archimedes' principle, I can still recite them off pat. Just don't ask me to spell them! Why is dyslexic one of the hardest words to spell? Were they trying to be funny?

Funnily enough, despite not really 'doing' school, I inherited from my parents a lifelong love of learning. Dinner table conversation growing up was always pretty highbrow and covered science, politics, history and philosophy. I never read at school, but as an adult I read lots and cover really varying topics, never fiction. I also travel a lot for fun and have been lucky enough to see the world – this exposure to new cultures and new people is great for personal development and understanding, and I feel like a real global citizen. It has even given me the courage to permanently live abroad. I no longer feel England is my home, but that the world is my home.

I believe when you stop learning you start dying.

The thing I really did love about school was the captive audience of willing buyers. Every day kids with pocket money were all around me, not to forget the teachers (they were the big fish in sales) and the school itself.

We used to receive a copy of *Industrial Exchange and Mart* – a magazine sent out to all farmers – and buried in the back there used to be adverts for stock disposal. One week I saw they had army surplus jumpers, £40 for 100. We had a school cadet force – the dressing up as soldiers department – so I went to see them and sold them ten for £40, which left me with 90 spare and already paid for. I swiftly sold them on to builders and scaffold workers.

Selling at school got even easier when I bought a cancelled export order of 2600 Cadbury's crème eggs. It was such a success that before long I was not taking any books, pens or school work with me in the mornings, just as many crème eggs as I could carry. Soon my enterprise was so big that the school tuck shop made a complaint. I was confronted by a teacher, who bought four packets, gave me a pat on the back and told me to try and be a bit more discreet.

The other thing I have to thank the school for was the career advice. My mother told me many years later that my careers officer had called her to say that she had never met a 14 year old who knew so absolutely what it was he wanted to do with his life. She said that I should just get on and do it. This must have really helped, as both of my parents were highly educated (my father has a Masters in organic chemistry) and as such had expected me to follow in their footsteps and go to university.

I cannot remember what I said to my careers advisor that day, but I suspect I just talked incessantly about whatever I was selling that week and how I was planning to make that into a huge multinational business.

Business Begins

I'd made my first tentative steps into business, but I still had a bedroom full of the remaining stock. Very kindly, my grandmother took me to a car boot sale to help sell some of it. This was a great success, so, when I was 14, I got a bit more serious and started my first business. Oasis Trading was based in one of the farm's sheds and operated at fairs, fetes and car boot sales. I picked up 100 pairs of second-hand jeans for £1 each. I bundled half of them into tens and sold them to other market traders, then sold what was left from my own stalls.

The moment I finished my last GCSE exam I never went back to school. I was 15 and running my own business – which soon expanded to a full-grown market stall and a productive channel selling surplus stock and over-buys to other traders. I had swiftly realised the value of bulk sales, so my costs were getting lower whilst I was also getting the extra sales from the other retailers I was supplying. It was a win–win situation.

However, entrepreneurs are like cats; whichever side of the door we are on we want to be on the other, and new ideas always take precedence in our mind over the activity we are currently engaged in – the new thing is way more interesting than the old thing.

Hence the appeal of an advert I came across one day, while looking for stock, for a fruit machine, on sale for £75. This seemed awfully cheap for a whole fruit machine, so I went to our local pub to find out what they paid for them. The landlord told me that they rent them for £15 a week. Now as a rental yield that is a pretty impressive return, but you have to remember I was only 15, so instead I agreed to sell it to him for £150. After a torturous trip to London to collect it – of course I couldn't yet drive so had to rely on my parents' help – the publican refused to take it. I was gutted.

In hindsight, imagine you are running a pub and a 15-year-old kid asks about your fruit machine and says he can get you one cheap. You probably don't expect him to actually come back with one. I guess I had not fully appreciated that some people still thought I was just a stupid kid.

This was a blow at the time, but it triggered a whole new business phase that inspired me to move out of the trading industry and into coin-operated machines. When I got home my mum reminded me that there was a bloomin' great fruit machine standing in the hallway of the house and that she wanted it removed. I grabbed *Yellow Pages*, turned to public houses and called them all.

I sold seven of the machines.

Of course I could have stopped at having sold one machine, as that is all I had in stock, but when you can see a marketing approach working, my advice is to keep sticking the bucket down the well until it comes up dry. This does of course create a problem of how to fulfil the order, but what a nice problem to have! This is a great lesson to learn: *always get the customer first; the rest will fall into place.*

This business was ideally suited to a kid; I bought the machines by phone, sold them by phone and customers would only find out I was 15 when I turned up. They were usually pretty surprised, especially if I had been giving them a hard time on prices over the phone. One client confessed that he wished his son would show some comparable initiative and took me under his wing, teaching me about the industry that I had blundered into.

I fulfilled my orders and offered my customers quiz and video games too, offering free installation and a share of the takings. Soon this new business, which I christened Oasis Leisure, had sites all over Dorset, aided by the fact that when I turned 17 I acquired a big red van and learned to drive. This transformed my reactivity. My dad was always great at taking me to the machines, but he worked long hours so it would often be late at night that we'd go to sites. The money was coming in and I was furiously busy, servicing, emptying and delivering machines, often single handed, sometimes with one of my mates in tow, just for the ride. I was the only one who bought rounds with ten pence pieces in the pub at night.

Then, one day I saw an advert for an amusement arcade for sale, in a major town centre in Somerset. This had instant appeal; it was only £30,000, it had a small takeaway business integrated with it and offered the hugely appealing detail that with all the machines in one place there'd be no more running around.

I approached my bank and, to my surprise, they lent me the money to buy it. So, at the ripe old age of 18, I moved to Somerset to run my own amusement arcade. Banks are obviously a lot more cautious nowadays and I apologise if I was in any way instrumental in that change of attitude.

What I had not fully appreciated was that the sites I had previously served were pubs, clubs and tourist attractions, and those businesses did marketing in order to find customers. What's more, I had used their heat, rent, light, rates and customers to fill my machines with money; now I had to find my own customers and cover the bills alone.

I lasted about a year. I lost everything and moved back in with my parents, a sheepish look on my face and my tail between my legs. I had failed – every would-be entrepreneur's worst nightmare.

I was a bit morose for a few weeks after this, but you know what? I still had all my arms and legs, nothing really serious had happened and it was a relief, at least, to be sleeping better. All the worry had taken its toll but, in the end, I was unhurt and not discouraged. I had started with nothing and I had nothing again, but what an experience – and, in hindsight, what a great age to go bust. A good kick in the nuts teaches you some humility at that age. Imagine how intolerable a human being I would have become if I had made a raging success of that arcade!

After this failure I was soon back on my feet and bristling with business ideas. I have always been the sort of person who can think of a few new ideas every day. Over the years I have learnt that a good idea scratches an itch and solves a real problem, not a problem that does not really exist. My way of testing the viability of a new business idea was often very simple. I would just go out and try selling it. This was similar to how I became involved in the fruit machine business. In that case what I did was to ring a load of people and try and sell the one machine that I had, which led me to realise that a readymade market existed to sell more machines. I have adopted the same policy to this day. As I have already said, find the customer first and then follow the customer by obtaining the goods that they want to buy. It is a steep learning curve, but if you cannot sell whatever it is you are thinking of selling, you are dead in the water, so it is best find out sooner rather than later.

Next I started a home improvement business, bringing customers and suppliers together. This is a really simple low cost business model you can apply to any industry. I simply approached a number of suppliers – for example, a company that sells conservatories – and agreed a commission on sales if I found them someone who wanted to buy. Essentially an agency agreement, the principle is that you sell their service under your own name, but they fulfil the delivery. In the industry it's often called white labelling. You can start a white label business or agency *TOMORROW*; you don't have to develop a product, you don't have to have stock and you don't even need particular expertise or equipment. Later, when I started my telecoms company, I began as simply a dealer or agent for other telecoms providers. This meant that for no real cost I could offer mobile phones, landlines, broadband and a whole host of other products. Then, as the business developed, I brought the successful services in house and offered them myself for a bigger margin.

This is a classic way to get started without over committing yourself. You basically just become a marketing channel for someone already established – and these companies are always looking for new sales, so it is a fairly easy conversation to have. I started the home improvement business purely because I met a guy who had a product, so I offered to sell it. In retrospect, I wasn't as focused as I needed to be, but I was learning fast.

The home improvements venture was swiftly followed with a franchised version of my original amusement arcade business. I would sell three machines on site for £1999, and it was, I soon discovered, pretty profitable. However, then I heard for the first time about pricing policies and test marketing prices. Basically the theory is that a small increase in your top line price is a big increase on your bottom line. In fact, in an average company, a 5% increase in your pricing can add 40% to your bottom line profit! When you consider that a business is often valued on a multiple of that annual profit (called a P/E or price/earnings ratio) then increasing it by 40% in one quick move is pretty dramatic. In fact you could afford to lose customers and still come out in front.

I made the decision, daring though it might sound, to change my pricing. I didn't alter anything except the price on the ticket, moving from £1999 to £2999, and guess what? My enquiry levels and sales levels didn't even blink. Writing this now, I am trying to figure out why I did not try putting those prices up again! I was probably so excited to find water in the well that I forgot to stick my bucket down again! Never mind – now at least I was making a real success of a business.

But, remember what I said about the restless spirit of entrepreneurs.

Mobile phones had just, for the first time, got appreciably small and inexpensive. I sensed an opportunity. I noticed a gap in the market, which very effectively served the needs of retail customers and provided a really high level of service to corporate customers but neglected all the small businesses in between, which were left out in the cold despite being intensive users of mobile phones.

So, I established a company called Unity to target this sector and started selling phones to businesses. We grew very quickly but were terribly undercapitalised so really had to run on a shoestring budget. But we grew and grew. When I sold the company in 2006 my combined businesses had a run rate turnover of about £13 million and 135 staff. And every single one was started with no money whatsoever. Every day things would go wrong, and every day things would go right. It was exciting and unpredictable.

My Epiphany

While I was running the telecoms company, I had an epiphany that changed my life and the way I do business forever.

The telecoms industry is very acquisitive, so as a new kid on the block, making lots of noise, we were often approached by other companies looking to buy us. Some of the approaches were dismissed out of hand; others were very tempting, but they had one thing in common – the companies didn't have any money, it was all 'jam tomorrow', predicted on a hypothetical event in the future that might never happen. But it got me thinking. Hang on, I have no money – maybe I could buy a business.

Now, something that ambitious could never be simple; the key was not just identifying a business that could be bought for no money, but rather finding a solution to a problem that really works for the seller and helps them to achieve what they want to do. I did my research, found a small mobile phone business whose problems I had a way of solving, and made my first acquisition. Not only did I grow my business, I grew it by about one year's sales in a single day.

All the books I had read reinforced my paradigm that in order to be successful you have to start a business and work really hard. I had done that over and again and yet here I had just cut out all the blood, sweat and years. It was as if instead of running the marathon I just ran the last ten yards but still got the trophy. This was my epiphany, and this is what I do now. I help companies that have some kind of problem that is motivating them to exit. I come up with a deal that will benefit us both, often when they have nowhere else to turn.

It is incredibly rewarding and enormous fun; and of course my paradigm now is not to start businesses but to buy them. However, that is another book for me to write, and something I can only do now because I learned to walk before I could run. You need to do the same. Starting your first business is a right of passage that every entrepreneur must go through, even if their ambitions are grander and loftier. Before you buy and sell businesses you need to understand all the warts and wrinkles of creating and running a company from scratch. You'll need to do that before you can ever empathise with someone whose business is struggling. You need to understand that logic gap between what should happen in business and what does happen, and you need to really feel what it is like in these situations.

The other realisation I had was that you make your money when you sell your business, not when you are running it. Running a business gives you income, and your expenses tend to grow to fit your income. Selling gives you capital; capital gives you real freedom and enables better decisions to be made, as well as providing you with time to make them.

Be customer-focused. Your best customer is the person who buys your business. Make it ready for that moment and for them alone, not for anyone else, making sure you sell while on the up not at the top. And sell as soon as you can. Doing it again with capital is much, much better.

And remember, at the heart of running a business is the art of doing a deal – get a feel for that now and there'll be no stopping you.

So here I am sitting in the beautiful Balearic Islands, buying and selling businesses that have problems and writing this book, and I realise what a long way I have come from setting fire to myself on a farm in Dorset. But I feel, at the age of 37, that I have four lifetimes worth of stories, knowledge and experiences, and I am really only just getting started.

I have been asked many times how I evaluate my ideas and what kind of paperwork and research is involved. The truth is that I don't tend to do much paperwork and more often than not I follow my own hunches and intuition. I tend to test the market by finding out whether something sells or not. If it does, then I continue with it as a business; if it doesn't, then I look for something that does. It really is as simple as that.

There is no right or wrong way to do this kind of thing; many people will do hours, even days, of research and planning before starting anything and I am sure that will reduce their chances of getting it wrong, but for me it would also lower the number of opportunities I have the time to exploit.

The best bit about all of this is that I thoroughly love what I am doing. I get up every day wanting to work and it provides me with great excitement and exhilaration. If you were to talk about work–life balance, then I believe that mine is perfect. I have learnt to focus my time on the areas that I am good at, which for me is the creative side and in making deals. I think it is important to start out doing everything in your business yourself. By doing this you will appreciate the need to understand it from start to finish and to change and tweak the various processes to get everything working right.

However, I am absolutely certain in my conviction that failure to focus on your strengths and let go of other aspects is what holds many businesspeople back. Many people doggedly hold on to a belief that if you want something done right you have to do it yourself. Indeed, often you will be the best person for the job, but *time is finite*, and so if someone else is only 50% as good then you may need to employ two people to do the job. If a business can't survive without your constant attention, you may have a more fundamental problem; a business that will enslave you to long hours and hard labour for life. It may be time to try something different.

I remember when I started my business, it was many years before I could afford my first holiday; that is, both afford in a financial sense and in terms of being able to be away from the office. This is a form of failure. You have quit your job and started your own business, but the objective was not to go into slavery!

You must be prepared to sacrifice, be prepared to struggle, but be sure to retain your enthusiasm and learn to treat the process like a game – failure is not so very bad that you can't bounce back and the reward is to free yourself completely – so it has to be worth it.

At one time I had to move into a student house to keep costs down, living on beans on toast sometimes for weeks at a time, as every penny went into growing the business. I remember days where I emptied the penny jar to put an embarrassingly small amount of petrol in the car I had borrowed, enough to be fairly sure I could get to the meeting but with no guarantee I could get back. I had no money for parking meters, so I'd have to try to hide the car somewhere it would not get a ticket.

It was a little frustrating at times, but never really played on my mind, it was just the way it was. I could see the business beginning to work and I was willing to give it everything – one shot, make it work. It is pretty character-building stuff to live like this and be master of your own destiny; no safety net. In a true meritocracy you get out what you put in.

I would not trade the experience for the world, without that experience I don't think I could fully appreciate what I have now. I still have a very real connection to the value of money, which is a very healthy thing to have.

You may have heard the expression 'I used to work for an idiot, now I work for a maniac'. If you haven't it'll come as no surprise to know it's used in reference to starting your own business.

I now live abroad and travel a lot, and it is important when you run your business to ensure it can function without you. Once it can, you know you've succeeded.

CHAPTER 2

Failure/Feedback/Risk

So what is it that holds people back from making that break? What is it that prevents them from starting a business that will generate wealth for themselves and their families, and contribute in a meaningful way to society in general?

Human nature means that we are affected by what other people think, and this carries huge weight in our decision-making process. In fact one of the biggest factors stopping people from making on-the-spot buying decisions is often their fear of what other people will think. Imagine you buy a new mobile phone and then go down the pub only to find out you bought an out-of-date model for too much money; the fear of being ridiculed for doing this type of thing is a very strong emotion and guides a lot of people's lives. This in turn can lead to driving procrastination and indecision. What if you start the business, it goes wrong and decisions you make are perceived by your peers to be naive or uninformed? What will everyone else think?

This understandable, very real fear manifests itself in people as a fear of failure and a fear of taking perceived risks.

So here are some thoughts for you to consider:

What is failure?
What is risk taking?

Think about this for a moment.

For me, failure would be to wake up in my old age, look back at my life and realise that I'd had the world at my feet but did nothing to improve my situation. That as a human being I had an equal chance in life to be the best version of myself possible but did not take it. I froze in the headlights and life passed me by.

Consider how it might feel to realise that you had spent your life being average and not fulfilling everything you could be.

When you are evaluating the risk of just doing it, why not try thinking of the risk of not doing it?

When you are, many years from now, sitting in your house with your grandchild on your knee, what will you tell them? What are you going to say, and how long will it take to say it? Will there, in telling the story of your life, be this big chunk of ten or 20 years in the middle that, on reflection, was pretty much the same except for the odd interruption of a much-needed holiday?

Read that again and really think about it.

Every day millions of people wake up in an average house in an average town, run past their 2.4 children whilst trying to down an impossibly hot cup of coffee at 7.30 am, then jump into a freezing cold car or catch a grossly overcrowded train. All to get to the office, work for eight and a half hours and then repeat the exercise in reverse. Every single day! This is a perfectly valid life choice for millions of people, and there is nothing wrong with it, but I am guessing that one of the reasons you bought this book is that you don't much want this life for yourself or for your family. You are reading this because you don't want to surrender to the momentum of mediocrity.

Success

Now, you don't have to run a business or make money to be successful; you could be the best mother, the finest musician or the greatest of friends to those that you love – but by making the effort to pick up this book you've demonstrated that you have the ambition to be an entrepreneur and run your own start-up. It's an ambition shared by lots of people, and there are various reasons why they might want to do it.

Consider what your reasons are.

Are they:

Money?
Do not be afraid of wanting money. A famous businessman and motivational speaker and trainer called Zig Ziglar once said, 'Money is not important, but it's right up there with Oxygen'. If you want to change the world, or your life, money gives you the ability and the opportunity to make choices. It can, of course, act as a negative force as well as a positive one, but without it you're deprived of the opportunity to choose that positive option, so it becomes a purely academic principle. Whatever you think of a desire for wealth, without it not many people will care what you think.

Recognition?
Your drive to succeed in business may derive from a desire to prove wrong people who have doubted you in the past, to show your old school bully or even your family that you are a more successful person than they think. Recognition could provide you with the impetus that will stroke your ego so that you become the envy of your peers. Oscar Wilde said, 'It is not enough to succeed in life; one must see one's friends fail'. A pretty awful sentiment but a bitingly accurate one that points to man's desire to be recognised amongst others as successful. There's nothing wrong with wanting others to appreciate you for your achievements.

Celebrity?
This is the next evolution of recognition – the desire to be loved and wanted by society as a whole. Most children now cite celebrity status as their primary ambition in life. We may consider this sad, but many celebrities are powerful and

inspiring. The *Dragons' Den* panel might not win any awards for good looks or singing ability, but they are recognised for their insight, intelligence, skill and cunning, and celebrity status like theirs can be a great force for good and for change in society. You will see over the next decade that the green movement and the drive for carbon reduction will be powered not by hippies with dogs on string, or old Etonians flapping on about third runways. It will be driven by bright dynamic entrepreneurs who will dream up businesses that will enrich the lives of people and, recognising how essential it is that their business models are environmentally friendly, the planet as well. So, just as being successful is nothing to be ashamed of, neither is being well known for it.

Lifestyle?

Some people are worried that a life in business will destroy their lifestyle, but if you are able to do what you want every day, and you are doing it for yourself, then you have won the game of life. Too many of us force ourselves to go through the motions in jobs we resent, failing to realise our desire to have more time, more control and less stress. A business run properly can provide you with freedom and choice for life. What kind of lifestyle is it you want?

Self-Satisfaction?

Wouldn't it be nice to live with the smug, self-satisfaction of knowing that you are the master of your own destiny; not answerable to anybody? Wouldn't it be comforting to know that everything you own you have created for yourself on your own terms? Imagine what it would be like to look in the mirror every day at a successful independent person; to be able to teach your children what it is like to truly master your own destiny and to have a full and rich life. Just think how well you'd sleep at night.

To Make a Better Life for Your Family?

You won't miss your children growing up; you can choose where you live and when you work; and you can leave your wealth behind for the next generation if you wish. Don't rely on selling your soul for 40 years as a wage slave, barely seeing your family just so you have enough money to scrape through your retirement. If you succeed you can provide a wonderful life for yourself and your family. And, even if things are tight and you cannot provide these things now, you will be teaching them really valuable lessons about determination and sticking with it, safe in the knowledge that things will come good if you fulfil your potential. What better lesson could you give to your children?

All of these things are benefits of pursuing the path you're considering. For me, failure would be to fail to take that challenge, to let life pass you by without ever enjoying any of the possible benefits of growing some balls and doing it for yourself.

Failure

You may have heard the expression 'There is no failure, only feedback'.

What that means is that you need to fail to learn. If you touch something hot, you'll burn your fingers, and the chances are you'll do everything in your power to avoid touching hot things again. Kids learning to walk will fall over repeatedly, but they will embrace this failure and try and try again because their desire to walk outweighs the fear of failure. If you can distil that raw ambition you had as a child and block out the bad habits you have picked up along the way from school and from your family, you can embrace the fear and do it anyway. Then, if you continue to keep trying again and again, without treating each failure as a cue to stop trying, this will merely be another lesson along the journey to success.

Sometimes it's good to admit to failure, but learn from the lessons and quickly start again. Failure is what you make of it; a disaster or just a temporary setback. Too many people are terrified of it, failing to understand that failure is often just a label imposed by a society lacking the imagination to appreciate the bravery of risk takers, or inspired by jealousy, directed by the risk-averse at people taking chances, who will one day be successful.

What happens if you do fail? Is it really that bad?

Isn't it better to have tried and failed, rather than to have never made the effort at all? Take a look at the success stories of today's top businesspeople and you will see that many of them failed with their first business ventures. But this didn't deter them from learning what caused them to fail, dusting themselves down and then starting all over again. There is nothing wrong in failing providing that you gain the resilience to try again.

There are plenty of examples to prove that you can triumph over failure and rise, like the Phoenix, from the ashes. Many years ago, when my amusement arcade business failed, I could never have imagined that now, with hindsight, I would regard this as a great experience. Today I am the sum total of all those experiences, and I would not trade them for the world. As this was my first big one, it hurt a little more, but had I known then what I know now, that I would dust myself down and do better the next time, I would have been far, far bolder in my endeavours. So I want to encourage you to just Go Do; don't look back and don't be afraid to fail – be afraid to stand still.

This brings me on to risk. People call me a risk taker. If you are in the police force, the army or the fire brigade you are a risk taker. Starting a business is not risky.

This is a point that always causes debate, because everybody thinks that starting a business is a risk.

You are taking a risk every time you climb into your car, every time you cross the road, every time you climb a ladder, every time you go abroad on holiday. You could die doing any of these things, but these are all risks that we seldom think about because they are the things we do every day as a matter of course. In short – life is a risk. If we didn't take a risk then we would be afraid to do anything in life. And consider this: it would be hard to die starting a business – unless you started an enterprise that involved testing parachutes!

Think about the fact that we are on this planet one time only (which is an assumption we may have to consider). The average life span – barring accident – is about 80 years, and the bald truth is that we're pretty useless for the first 20 years and powering down towards the end. The reality is that we have an average period of 40 years of the really good bit in the middle; the productive time. When you think of it in those terms, something you do for ten years, like my telecoms company, is 25% of the vital period of your life! It's a chastening thought, and enough to make us look back at our life and wonder what we were thinking devoting so much time to such a narrow set of experiences. But those ten years, in my case, were valuable and I learned and earned from the experience. Plenty of us do the same job for ten or 20 years, operating a small fraction of the total business function within our job area, repeating that fragment of experience over and over, groundhog day style. Is that what you want for yourself?

If you Go Do, you may lose some money, you may feel like you have wasted some time and you may have a boom–bust roller coaster of a life, but when you are looking back you will have had the most magnificent journey. Life is not about accumulating stuff – it is for living, for adventure, for happiness and satisfaction. Will you find that in a nine-to-five office job?

Will you discover that in your eagerness to fit in with the conventional story, you are just a blur in a suit in the rush hour squeeze? Would you prefer to spend your time watching life pass by while you rush around, working your balls off for an employer who doesn't appreciate your efforts? Or would you prefer to run your life by your own set of rules, and be completely in control of your own destiny?

Failure, Success, Risk and Reward are all relative.

People see business as a tightrope walk with failure and despair on either side. What if I told you the tightrope was only six inches off the ground?

I have been through the mill financially on many occasions. I have had weeks where every letter was a final demand or a court summons, and every phone call a debt collector.

I have struggled with arrears and debts that by most people's standards would scare them to death: but you have to think in life, 'what is more important?' Do you focus on all the short-term issues and problems, or do you focus on your outcome, ignore the trivia (and it really is trivia) and just keep going towards your goal?

So don't risk doing nothing with your life, grab life by the scruff of the neck and give it a good shake, challenge yourself every day and enjoy the journey.

The Lessons to be Gained from this Chapter

- Don't be afraid to follow your instincts.
- Concentrate on getting the customers – once you have them *only then* turn your attention to obtaining whatever they are asking you to supply.
- You're never too young – or too old – to start a business but procrastination burns up valuable time.
- Have fun by doing what you want to do.
- Learn from your early mistakes – and try not to repeat them.
- Sometimes you need to fail to learn – but don't treat failure as an excuse to stop trying.
- Remember that failure is not yet a crime – if you fail, pick yourself up and start afresh.

- Concentrate on what you are good at and, whenever possible, delegate what you are not good at once you have experienced how to do it yourself.
- Learn as much about all aspects of your business as you can.
- Do not be influenced by the negative views of other people.
- Time is finite.

CHAPTER 3

GO YOU!

So you have heard my story – now it is time to start yours.

I was lucky enough to have an upbringing that showed me that I could more or less do as I liked and it would all be okay.

My father has many expressions, but an apt one at this point is: 'They'll never let you starve'.

What it means is: What is the worst that can happen? What can go wrong if you start doing something for yourself and it doesn't work? It certainly won't kill you, it will definitely change your life one way or another, and it could just catapult you into fabulous wealth. For most people it will be their best chance of making a decent amount of money.

I really believe that the only way you are ever truly likely to make a comfortable living is to take control of your own destiny by starting a successful business.

Of course, everybody has their own ideas about what is a 'comfortable living'. My idea of this is to be in a position where I make enough money to be financially secure for the rest of my life.

Many of us look forward to retirement as a time when we are able to wake up in the morning and do whatever we want. It's an appealing definition, so little wonder we look forward to it so much. But what happens if we turn the phrase around? In other words, if every day you wake up and do exactly whatever you want, are you already retired? I think it is important to look at life's journey in these terms and to get away from the idea that you work your whole life and defer your enjoyment until old age and the conventional definition of retirement. You need to ensure that what happens in your daily life is special, important, memorable and fulfilling – and not just a process of filling in time until you finally get to enjoy the fruits of your labour. The number of people who spend all day, every day, in an office looking at Facebook and doing a bit of work is truly frightening.

In NLP (Neuro-Linguistic Programming) there is an expression for one of the levels of learning. It is called 'unconscious competence'. The idea is that when you start a new process, like driving a car, you start out as:

Consciously incompetent

This means that you think about it consciously, but you are incompetent – so, not very good at it but expending effort and trying to improve.

You then become:

Consciously competent

By this stage you're a driver. You're fully qualified, you know how to drive, and when you concentrate you can do all of the necessary parts of the process competently.

Finally, when you get really good and well practised you become

Unconsciously competent

This means you can perform the task or process in pretty much auto pilot. It means you have done it so many times that it becomes second nature and you can effectively switch off and just perform the task. To use the driving analogy, you may be midway through a long journey and suddenly notice that you have come quite a long way along the route, so far that you don't remember every part of the journey or each junction you missed on the motorway. You're able to drive effectively without needing to consciously concentrate.

I have a belief that you can become unconsciously competent at life – you do the same thing every day, same journey to work and same job, and as such you get really good at it. Then, because you're on autopilot, you find that you have missed a bunch of junctions. Only these junctions are not on the M25, they are the years you have on this planet and you discover that life is flying past you while you competently, but unconsciously, whizz through your time on this earth.

So please stop – and shake it up. Consider the journey you're undertaking and the alternatives in front of you. Time passes a lot faster when you're in a state of unconscious competence. It's time to learn some new tricks, push yourself onward and put some learning back into your life. You'll find that, all of a sudden, you're noticing things more, taking more opportunities and actively participating in your life, rather than being an effective passenger. Your life will literally last longer as a result.

Limiting Beliefs

The biggest single barrier most people have is their own set of limiting beliefs – a suspicion or a conviction that they are not good enough or smart enough or brave enough. We are all plagued with doubts and insecurities about our capabilities. We will never find out just what we can do until we give it a go, but because of our limiting beliefs we're reluctant to try.

When you are a child you believe anything is possible. That's why you learn to walk and talk, and why you have a burning desire to progress. As a child, you also have absolutely no experience of failure to fall back on. But as you get older you are influenced by school, society and family and encouraged to believe that life is a struggle and that some things are simply not possible.

How Do You Break This Down?

To do so you must first start believing in yourself, in your capacity to take on a new challenge and to succeed against the odds. Now, annoyingly, the first thing that you try will, in all probability, not turn out how you want. You may choose to perceive that as a failure, but I really hope by the end of this book you realise that the real failure is not failing in pursuit of something worthwhile, but failing to do and failing to try. The lessons you will learn along the way may be hard, and they may hurt, but you should wear a smile safe in the knowledge that you are really living. And if you are humble and show humility then you will not have set huge expectations with friends and family; your pedestal will not be so high as to make the fall painful.

Start off being positive about what you intend on doing and most of all don't listen to the negative advice that you are almost certain to hear from others. Unless they have great experience in the area you are looking to work in, their advice may not be useful anyway.

Do you remember the Oscar Wilde quote from earlier, 'it is not enough to succeed in life; one must see one's friends fail'? Well, unfortunately, this means that even your closest loved ones may be discouraging, not always because they think you can't do it, but often because they are worried that you can – and your success would expose their own lack of ambition and bravery. It is human nature to compare ourselves to our peers, and often people would sooner run another down than see their own lack of gumption revealed.

People often say how lucky I am – and I am lucky – but I chose my life, I made my luck, and I firmly believe that all other adults can make similar choices and experience similar success, and must not blame others if they don't take that first step.

> 'So many other people have strived through adversity that it will embarrass you'
>
> Colonel Sanders of KFC

When Colonel Sanders was *65 years old* he received his first social security cheque of $99. He was broke. His only asset was a secret chicken recipe.

He left his home in Kentucky and travelled to the many states in the US to try to sell this recipe. He offered his secret chicken recipe to many restaurants for free; all he wanted in return was a small percentage of the sales. However, he was shown the door by most of the numerous restaurants he called on.

'Get out of here. Who wants a recipe from a white Santa Claus?' the restaurant owners shouted, referring to the dress code Sanders adopted: a white shirt and white trousers. Over 1000 restaurants rejected his offer. How many of you would have quit after making one or two unsuccessful sales calls?

On his 1009th sales visit, one restaurant finally accepted his offer.

Today, Kentucky Fried Chicken outlets and fatherly Colonel Sanders statues are found all over the world.

Colonel Sanders succeeded against the odds because he nurtured a positive belief in himself and in the secret recipe that he had developed. He refused to be intimidated and he was not prepared to accept defeat for his idea.

The Kentucky Fried Chicken story is just one example of how one person's desire to succeed consumed him. Surely there were many who watched his efforts and despaired, assuming that he would never find a buyer for his recipe. But his perseverance paid off, and in the business world there are thousands of other stories about men and women who had the determination and strength to follow their dreams.

You Need to Have Resilience

Search the web or go to the library and research other businesses that have become extremely successful. You'll find that the majority will have been started by an individual, who, like you, wanted more from life than a nine-to-five existence.

James Dyson provides another great example. Dyson completely re-invented the vacuum cleaner, a revolutionary bit of design that was only the first of numerous incredible successes. However, Dyson had to overcome all kinds of adversity before his success was realised. His book *Against the Odds* should be one of the first books on your reading list when you have finished this one.

What these people are telling us, if you read between the lines of their remarkable stories, is that they are not prepared to take 'no' for an answer.

Limiting beliefs are the self-deprecating words we use when we tell ourselves we cannot do things.

'I can't swim'

'I can't speak French'

'I can't just start my own business'

There is one short answer to this: If other people can, why can't you?

It really is as simple as that. You are no different, no luckier or less lucky, no less intelligent. In fact many people without education often start businesses because they are tired of being rejected for sensible employment. For all that an education is hugely worthwhile, having an examination pass certificate only really proves that you have the ability to put down on paper what the examination adjudicators want you to say. Just as having qualifications is absolutely no guarantor of success, having no formal qualifications cannot be used as a valid reason for not doing what you want to – but it is frequently used as an excuse for procrastinating. If you really want to be successful then you must accept that formal qualifications and established knowledge bases do not 'maketh the man' and force yourself to do something and learn something new in order to generate the life you want.

I know of two multi millionaires who cannot read or write, and it has never held *them* back. Plenty of people with dyslexia and those excluded from school are often found in the ranks of the rich and famous. There is no link other than the fact that they had to find another path to make their way in life.

Throughout history, religious or ethnic minorities have been discriminated against in the workplace but this hasn't prevented them from going out and starting their own businesses. Prime examples of this are The Quakers who have become successful business owners.

Sometimes, in fact, the more you stay in education the more you are encouraged to conform to what society wants, because the people teaching you, for all their knowledge, are amongst the least entrepreneurial people in the world. They are merely another example of the fact that we must question the lessons we are taught, the advice we are given and the assumptions that we hold. Limiting beliefs serve no useful purpose and do nothing but hold us back. What are your limiting beliefs? Don't you think it might be time to overcome them?

Taking Away the Safety Net

Have you ever thought that if there wasn't a safety net and you were a tightrope walker, you'd probably get quite good at what you were doing pretty quickly? The fear of falling would certainly focus the mind!

Well, you need to get rid of the safety net in life too. There is nothing like needing the money, or needing to prove yourself to those who doubted you, to help you find a way. The key is to harness that necessity and transform it into desire, use it positively rather than negatively. If you respond in the wrong way you will become the panicky desperate rabbit that gets caught in the headlights. If you respond the way I want you to, you'll learn fast and succeed before you know it.

In Napoleon Hill's famous book *Think and Grow Rich* he talks about having a burning desire. Without such a desire you cannot have the mindset to achieve the things that are foremost in your list of wants.

You may think you know what your burning desire is, but it is often different. Your desires are manifested by your actions, so what you do, say and how you act defines your desire.

You may think you want to make money, but your actions show that you put watching football or television first. You may nurture a desire to shed some extra pounds or to become physically fitter, but the fact that you merely talk about it rather than attending the gym testifies to the fact that you're content to allow your waistline to continue expanding. Despite our best intentions, our actions betray our unconscious minds, and the gym scenario, for example, is exactly why so many people join but never get beyond their first few visits.

These actions are the response of your unconscious. Your conscious mind thinks you want to start a business, but your unconscious psyche thinks you should choose the path of least resistance. Your conscious mind knows you need to devote some time to planning your business when you get home from work, but your unconscious psyche craves that bottle of wine or early night. There is nothing wrong with either of those cravings, but neither will make you rich. An inability to exert discipline on your unconscious psyche is perfectly understandable and something we all struggle with at one point or another. Therefore, you have to train your mind in order to enable your conscious thoughts to begin to take the upper hand.

Do You Want to Change?

I run lots of businesses and I am involved in lots of things all the time. Staying focused on the things I need to do in order to take me to the next stage of my business development can be tricky. So, I do certain things in order to make things happen in the way that I want them to. I am going to let you in on a little trick that can really help you in achieving a goal.

Get a big bit of paper and a pen. Write the following at the top.

> *I want to start a business because* . . . . . (you can use this for any goal of course)

Now write 200 reasons and do not stop until you have finished.

Sounds silly? Well, so is wanting to start a business and not being willing to get started on it, so bear with me – there is method in my madness. What my little exercise does is to really engage your brain by forcing you to take a moment to write things down. How did you learn when you were at school? You learnt by writing things down. You wrote down what the teacher had told you and you copied what was written on the blackboard. Writing is a powerful tool for focussing the mind and fixing on ideas clearly. By writing so many reasons for wanting to start your business, you will exhaust your conscious mind, but there is no need to worry, because this in turn will cause your unconscious mind to become activated.

As a result your unconscious side will now begin to develop a more pro-active approach towards your desire to become successful. You are forcing the negative side of your mind to think of more and more reasons for getting your business started immediately, in direct contradiction to its previous instinct, which told you to procrastinate. You will start to realise that the favourable points are being reinforced as you effectively repeat the questions over and over again.

'Repetition is the mother of learning' (Repeticio est mater studiorum)

St Thomas

When writing down your list of reasons it does not matter how silly or random the reasons are, or even how similar they may be, because they will all have relevance.

You may say: 'I want to run my own business because:

'I want money to visit Australia'
Then you may add later: 'I want to go to Sydney'

'I want to go to Perth'

'I want to watch the Melbourne Grand Prix' and so on.

It really doesn't matter as long as you just get your brain really thinking about what you want and start luring your unconscious to join in and begin to support, rather than undermine, your desires.

It may sound tedious and silly, but believe me it is a very powerful and simple way of changing your mindset and putting you on the path to achieving your goals. It provides you with the means to learn and develop constantly.

Learning must never be underestimated – a pound invested in your head is worth ten in your pocket. I left school when I was 15 because a standard education didn't meet my needs – I made the decision that further education could not offer me greater benefits than the experience of learning for myself, something I would do by following my instincts, making some real life mistakes, travelling the world and reading about people who have achieved some of the things I wanted to achieve. So I found alternative ways to learn and, even if you don't share my views about conventional education, you can continue to expand your horizons and follow my path.

There is no shortage of insightful information at your fin-gertips. Over the years I have read hundreds of books, attended training courses, seminars and keynote speaker presentations, and learned a lot along the way.

Just look at what is out there:

Books – 'How to' books on your field of business; biog-raphies of successful people, or other great figures in history. Switch your reading habits to relevant reading.

Magazines – Your industry magazine is a must and there are a lot of good business titles out there too. When you are relaxing you'll gain far more by reading something like this than by vegetating in front of the television.

The internet – Research your competitors; research other businesses in different fields which target the same customers; learn how they sell; how they promote themselves; how you found them; which ones failed to inspire you causing you to move to another web site; which site you stopped to read. When you have done this, stop and consider why you stopped to read some and why you skipped past others.

Seminars and training – Most training organisations and personal development speakers offer very cost effective, or even free, seminars, so they can give you a taste of what they do and potentially sell you something more. These are great value and if the bigger picture is relevant it is well worth considering the investment.

Meeting people – You need to be open in life if you are going to make your own journey. So network like crazy. The more you listen, the more you learn: appreciate that everybody has a story; some will be a waste of time others will be pure gold. Get out there and learn from everyone. Be a student of the world.

The Lessons to be Gained from this Chapter

- Believe in yourself.
- Have resilience and never take no for an answer.

- Do not allow a lack of formal qualifications to stand in your path.
- Take away your safety net and learn to make your own way in life.
- Train your subconscious mind to act positively.
- Engage your brain by writing down your 200 reasons for wanting to start your own business.
- Learn as much as you can from the 'University of Life' by reading, listening and seeing what other entrepreneurs have managed to achieve.

CHAPTER 4

THE WORST FIVE EXCUSES

So what is holding you back and why haven't you started? Sometimes those who procrastinate have the best of intentions, but saying you will do it – but not today – is almost as bad as pretending you don't want to do it in the first place. Procrastination leads to the death of ideas; only action sets you free.

Having talked to a number of people and analysed what common ideas hold people back the most, I quickly discovered that there are five top excuses people tend to use; five excuses that repeatedly prevent people from taking action. Let's go through them and explore their validity.

Excuse 1: I Need a Lot of Money to Start a Business

This is the most common excuse, and the most common misconception.

I often come across businesses that are run by people who waited half their life to start a business, not taking the leap until they had accumulated significant life savings. Then, wrongly thinking their savings represent a safety net, they proceed to lose the lot. The ones that pick themselves up and start again often get it right by starting a business with no money the second time around. Others will give up and go back to corporate life furiously stuffing as much as they can into a pension, admitting defeat and giving up on their dreams.

I believe that in your first business it is inevitable that you will waste a lot of money, no matter how much you plan. The business world is an imperfect model that changes constantly and you have to be truly dynamic with your decisions and actions. Unless you are extremely lucky and manage to get by without making any errors, it is likely that you will take a few wrong turns or go down a few dead ends, and these mistakes all cost money.

Far better to start with nothing, with nothing to lose, and you will be amazed at how resourcefully you can stretch a zero budget. I have started virtually every business I've created with nothing. If I had lots of capital I could no doubt have grown quicker. Conversely, in some cases, I could have lost a fortune – but you have to play the cards you are dealt and get on with it.

It is possible to start a business in almost any industry without capital. It would be really useful to have £500, but not essential. A phone and a brain are pretty much the only pre-requisites in my experience – and I have seen it done without the latter (but rarely without the former!).

You may think you need all sorts of things to get started. For example, I had a meeting with someone recently who wanted to invest a fortune to get his corporate image right, his website right, his offices and staffing right, but he had not even considered finding a customer first! He is in for a bumpy ride. He may become very successful, but you cannot put the cart before the horse. I could mention countless business start-ups that have failed because the founders had prioritised their own status and image before thinking about finding some customers.

The customer – this is a business saying that really is true – is king. You may have to blag a little and bluff a little more, but concentrate on the customer above and beyond all other things. The customer comes first. Having a pile of orders to fulfil is a lovely problem to have – trust me. You need to start somewhere and the first step is telling people what you do. I love the expression 'fake it 'til you make it'. Every business out there had a first customer once upon a time, so don't panic and worry. The good news is that you can find a customer without a budget. Once again, a phone and a brain will see you through.

You will find a way. What you must *NOT* do is to make an excuse for putting it off. People tend to get stuck in a 'chicken and egg' situation and they don't look for customers in the belief that they must have the product *before* finding them. They procrastinate because they haven't got the money to buy the product in the first place and this stops them from bothering to find the customers that will buy it.

Look at it another way: say you went out and spent several thousands of pounds on products that nobody wanted – where would that leave you? You would be seriously out of pocket and up the Suwannee without a paddle! It is far better to make sure that you have the customers in place *before* you outlay a load of money; once you know you have somebody to buy your product then the money will flow in as you make your sales. It is quite a logical philosophy really.

As I have already said, too many people make the excuse that they can't start a business without having the money to buy their stock. However, it is more important to source where your customers are going to come from before even thinking of supplying them.

Take the example of a man I know who runs a successful PR agency. He started out in business when he got talking to a lady at a horse racing event. By demonstrating a great business skill – listening – he discovered that the biggest challenge she faced in her line of work concerned PR people letting her down and not delivering on what she wanted; or more specifically failing to deliver what they had promised to deliver. My colleague had never done PR in his life – he was basically a salesman – but he offered to sort it out for her. As a result the lady became his first client and from that day forward he became a PR man.

Years later when they were having dinner, the lady said 'That first day we met; you didn't have a clue about PR did you?' Somewhat taken aback, he admitted the fact and she congratulated him on having the balls to blag the business. She also acknowledged something vital; that his determination not to let her down meant he delivered far more than the expensive agencies she had used in the past. This provides a very useful insight into what makes a business work. If you put the needs of your customer first, you won't go far wrong – budget or no budget.

You can even take on a client at cost, explain to them that you want to use them to develop your offering and use them for references, so in exchange you offer them a really good deal. This first customer might already be in your mobile phones contact list. Interesting thought!

Some people become obsessed with having all of their ducks in a row before they start. For me there is only one duck that matters: your first paying customer. Get that right and the rest will surely follow. People just love coming up with reasons why they won't do it, and there are few things I love more than coming up with reasons why they can – and this is a prime example.

Of course, some businesses have a higher financial barrier to entry than others. For example, you might want to own your own night club. Well clearly that *will* require capital, but many of the big club owners today started by promoting an event. This is done by putting on an event in someone else's club and building from there. If you do this and you do it well then you start to build an army of loyal followers. Once again, the customer comes before the showcase.

This is often the way that many rock bands start out if they have any savvy and want to make it big. They may hire a small venue or even play for free in a local pub or club. If they are any good they gradually build a loyal number of fans who spread the word. The band then moves up the ladder and plays at slightly bigger venues and, if they continue to interest their followers, their success will grow as a result. Imagine what would happen if a totally unknown band was to fork out a vast sum of money to hire Wembley Stadium; nobody would turn up. Buying and selling is really based very much on a snowball effect that relies on increasing sales to create the momentum.

Similarly, you might decide to start a telecoms company and take on Vodafone. Well, that's no mean feat even with capital, so getting creative is the best way forward.

In the most simplistic of terms: 'walk before you run'. You will be amazed how many people forget this basic rule.

If you can show you can perform it is easy to raise money later from investors or banks, but don't start looking for the money first, make that phase two.

Think about *Dragons' Den* again; only the guys who have their first customer and are showing promise get the money. People who want money for stock or marketing are regularly laughed off the show, or told to get out there and get some orders first.

Other ways to enter businesses with high entry costs include becoming an agent. For example, you might want to start a telephone company. Well, you can't become Vodafone over-night, but Vodafone might let you sell its services under an agency agreement. Or, if you have specific skills, such as accountancy or sales, you could partner with someone who also wants to start a business and share resources. I am a big fan of joint ventures of this kind – tactical partnerships that will help you achieve your goals.

Contacts are by far and away more important than money. So start talking to people, tell them your plans, share your dreams and make a point of getting out there to promote yourself. You will be amazed how the pieces of the jigsaw start to slot together when you really start to talk about it and work towards it.

If you do really need money to get going, then there are a few options that you can use to leverage OPM (other people's money):

1. **The three Fs** – Friends, Family and Fools. This is a slightly light hearted way to put it, but if you are really determined and even after considering all that I've said you still need a few quid, it is acceptable to beg. Draw up a one pager with what you want and what you will offer. Do you want debt (you will pay it back) or equity (they will have a share in the business)?

2. **Creditors** – These are companies or suppliers. Often you can agree to deal with a company exclusively or do a deal to get terms from a supplier to pay them later. This allows you to trade first and pay for the products later, although as a new business they may ask for guarantees. Avoid providing these if possible. In the main, people still like dealing with people so make personal contacts to explain what you are doing and how you would like their support with an account. Win them over with your passion and integrity. When it comes to being guarantor to your company's debts, remember a guarantor is an idiot with a pen.

3. **Taxman** – A strange one I know, but it is possible to charge customers for VAT and then pay your VAT quarterly. If you are a small business you can use something called flat rate VAT, or even annual accounting, so that you can benefit from holding on to the tax for a bit longer. This is interest free money. Ask your accountant for options. They will no doubt tell you to be careful, because should you be late paying you will be in trouble and the penalties imposed

are likely to be exceptionally high. But hey, if your business doesn't work you are in trouble anyway, so in for a penny in for a pound. Besides, if you start by talking negatively you will soon prove yourself right.

4. **Credit cards** – Not good for long-term funding but useful when getting started, particularly for bridging. For example, you might have to buy a stock item in for someone who has pre-ordered – so this method of payment could be useful. Beware, you are not supposed to use credit cards for business purchases, so don't tell them and, more specifically, don't tell them I told you not to tell them!

5. **Invoice finance** – Ask your bank about this. It is not particularly cheap but when you are growing it enables you to lay your hands on up to 80% of the value of your invoices. This can keep your business going when you have lots of money out there waiting to come in but you need to finance your payroll or next order etc.

6. **Payroll finance** – This is relatively new, but is very useful in businesses where the key commodity is people, such as in IT, call centres, engineer based businesses etc. Companies which are involved with this type of financing pay your staff for you for two months, which can assist with your cash flow, particularly during the early days of your business. You then start paying back in month three. This enables you to expand by providing you with breathing space in your cash flow to get the staff up to speed by billing for their time.

7. **Employees** – You can often take on key personnel, or even normal members of staff, and ask if they would like to invest in shares in the business. You would be

surprised what people sometimes have tucked away for a rainy day and giving staff a piece of the action can really help with buy in and confirm their loyalty towards the business. There are pitfalls attached to this, so ensure that you get proper legal advice first.

8. **Partners** – Can your partners invest, or can you offer investment to suppliers? You will need to produce a 'what is in it for them' document to provide sound reasons why they should invest in you. I successfully raised the funding for a business once by getting a supplier to invest. This was not done by putting in cash, but by provision of the core product the company was selling. So, instead of paying cash for the stock we needed, we were able to pay for it with shares in the company. This was a tidy little arrangement because the company got the benefit of a tame customer without having to part with hard cash. In return we received the equivalent of cash and we managed to establish a great relationship with our supplier.

9. **Asset finance** – If you need money to buy a van, a computer or some other tangible, and you cannot get a loan as you have no security, asset finance or lease finance provides the security in the item you are buying.

10. **Finally the bank** – Good luck with this one! I have no particular advice here but it is like getting blood out of a turnip. If you can give them £100,000 in cash and the keys to your house you can probably get a small overdraft. Okay this is a terrible exaggeration, but bank facilities are a bit of work in the early days, and pretty thankless to boot. They also tie you up in so many knots they preclude just about any other

form of finance. You might have guessed what my advice is here: if there is an alternative to the banks then take it. In recent years the banks that were once regarded as the 'honest John' pillars of society have lost much of their credibility. It has often been said that the banks will provide you with an umbrella while the sun is shining, but as soon as it rains they will take it back. This has repeatedly been proved to be very true.

In short, you can probably do without. I did, many have, and made a virtue of building from nothing. There's less to lose and plenty to gain – so join the club!

Excuse 2: I Cannot Afford to Leave Work

When starting a business, the first question you need to come to terms with is: do you need to leave work? You need to think about whether you can get this business set up in your spare time – that might sound like an intimidating prospect, but perhaps it's not so impossible if you take a week's holiday to really devote to the set up. And, are you starting with a business partner or do you have a supportive life partner such as your spouse? Things may not be as hard as you assume.

Finding time may not be as difficult as you suppose. In the early days of starting a business you must expect to sacrifice a bit of your social life to invest the time in your new venture. Do you realise if you watch two hours of television a day that comes to no less than 30 whole 24-hour days a year? This equates to 19.4 normal working weeks of 37.5 hours. So you need to consider knocking the TV on the head in order to plan and develop your business instead. Isn't it surprising just where the time goes when you are sitting in front of that TV? A 19-week period is not so far off half a year, glued to absolute garbage on a flashing box, as opposed to taking control of your life and really getting somewhere – no wonder it's called the idiot box! Find time that you're already wasting and all of a sudden getting a business started outside of conventional working hours does not seem so impossible.

If you do have a job currently, and if you are at all serious about starting your own business, then you may have to have an element of crossover. That doesn't mean abusing your employer's time, but there may be a reasonable way to use your free time in the office and utilise its resources in an acceptable fashion. Of course, if you take it too far and your employer sacks you for a bit of moonlighting then it crystallises your decision, does it not?

So before you panic and assume you need to give up your job, first think about how you can fit your business around your work:

- Can you deal mainly online and just check emails?
- Can you get a telephone answering service to take messages for you and make sure the phone is answered by a real person?
- Can you operate evenings and weekends, for example, market trading, consultancy etc.?
- Can you prepare everything you need while at work and then make the step across into your enterprise once you feel the time is right?

- Do you have a partner who can stay in work and support you in the early stages or do you need to stay in work and support your partner?

That's not to say that you shouldn't rule out taking bolder action. Let's consider the reality of taking the decision to just pack in the job and go for it. Do you know how hard it is likely to be to replace your salary?

Depending on what you plan to sell, it is remarkably easy to replace your income. A salary of £25,000 a year is only £500 per week. If you think about where you work now, they will probably be generating five times that at least from your productivity! In fact, if you are not generating this sort of revenue for your current employer, you should be looking to start your business sooner rather than later because your days could be numbered. So what we give to our employer in relation to what we get back is eye-opening stuff. Why not generate that money for yourself?

If your fear of leaving work is being overcome by your fear of failing in business and then having nothing, it may help you to rationalise your thoughts. If you do start your own business, get it wrong and the business closes down, you may find that mortgage repayments and the like will force you to look for alternative employment before you try and start a business again. If you do, reporting that your last job was as the MD of your own business on your CV will only reflect well on your ambition and guts, and may well push you a good way up the career ladder if you do decide to look for a conventional job again.

I employ several people in my various businesses that have previously worked for themselves and I can honestly say that they have brought a wealth of experience and knowledge to my organisations. Most business leaders worth their salt will take a similar approach, and, while some may adopt the narrow minded view that anyone that they employ who had previously had their own business may decide to steal their customers and start up their own thing all over again, all I can say is that such a defensive view cannot reflect a great deal of confidence in the strength of their own company.

The decision to stick with your job or go it alone is yours to take and yours alone; it may be prudent and possible to start this business up while you're still in full employment, and if so that's a great way to get started, but don't be afraid of making the leap – starting afresh and with only yourself to answer to is what this is all about, after all.

Excuse 3: I Heard 80% of New Businesses Go Bust in the First Three Years

This is a familiar excuse, and it is an understandable concern to voice. In fact, it gets worse – a further 80% of the remaining businesses fail in the following two years. It is rational to worry when reading that statistic. But here's a counterbalance: 80% of multi millionaire entrepreneurs have failed at least once.

I believe that a number of businesses fail because people simply give up. They start the business out of a romantic notion that it will not be challenging and as soon as they experience some pressure they go straight back to work.

I have stared down the barrel of failure more times than I can count, but I have only actually been there twice, and even then I do not consider them failures, just aspects of the journey that were a little 'off piste'. For all the pain they caused at the time, they taught me great lessons that have led me to where I am today. Just like in the film *Sliding Doors*, some days you get on the train and some days you miss the train; either way you are where you are and you should never regret the path that you took if it has resulted in you being where you are today.

In life you simply have to accept that there will be challenges and you will have setbacks, but the degree of these setbacks is often only in the eyes of the beholder. I am very circumspect about my challenges. Some people have had far greater setbacks on their journeys into business, while others have had very minor challenges. The former often remain convinced that the world and all its inhabitants get up every morning determined to hold them back from their endeavours. You must learn to accept that the world isn't against you; you are the ultimate controller of your own destiny and it is your own mindset that frequently controls your path.

You have to think about failure as a learning experience. If you start with nothing and in two years you end up with nothing, but have amassed an awesome CV and a whole wealth of experience, then the next time you'll use that experience wisely and will crack it. By way of comparison, two years in the same job for an employer is only likely to give you a few more grey hairs.

I can't tell you that the prospect of starting a business that may fail is not intimidating, but failed businesses aren't the end of the story. Look at those multi millionaires who learned from their mistakes and got back on the horse: I bet they have few regrets. And don't forget that one of the great benefits we have in the UK is legislation that protects you from total financial loss, if you ring fence your business through a limited liability company. By doing this you only risk the capital you invest. To find out about the ways to structure your company you should ensure that you take advice from an accountant or your local Business Link advisor when you first start.

If you are fortunate, then you could find that you are one of the people that do get it right first time; many do. Remember that the odds of succeeding in your first business venture are loads better than your chances of winning the lottery. To succeed in gaining true freedom you have a one in five chance of making your business succeed, and if you stick at it, a rich life full of adventure can be your reward!

However, you need to learn to embrace failure as a learning exercise. There is a training technique in cold calling that tells you to learn to love the word *NO*. This is because every time a sales prospect utters the word 'no' it will bring you one step closer statistically to one that will say 'yes'. You just need to keep smart, work hard and learn your lessons. Most importantly, if you know what you are doing and why you are doing it, there will be no need to give a monkey's about what other people think. Failure and success can both be found on the two sides of the same line. Just make sure you do right by people, and do not leave a trail of debris.

If you set out tomorrow and decide you are going to be an entrepreneur, then you must appreciate that at times you will be agreeing to suffer the rough with the smooth. Sometimes things will be better than on other occasions and you may alternate between being rich and poor. Nothing is certain in this life, but taking risks opens us up potentially to much richer and more satisfying rewards, and richer experiences. In my business career I have found that you need the lows to fully appreciate the highs – a life with a real mix of emotions is a full life indeed.

Excuse 4: I Need to Gain More Experience in My Chosen Field before Making the Leap

This is such a common excuse, which I believe is rooted in the way people have developed a knack of saying they are going to start a business in order to simply sound like the person they want to be. What most tend to do is to put it far enough in the future as to defer taking any actual action and, therefore, avoid the potential of failure and the ridicule of society that could occur if they go ahead and realise their goals.

The usual reasoning is something like this:

> *'I work for a PR company; I am going to stay here for another five years and really learn the business and then start my own agency'. Let me ask you this: Where on earth would you get more experience than by actually running the business?*

Think about it for a moment. If the person contemplating starting their own business, in the same field in which they are already employed, is aged, say, 25, what will happen if they procrastinate? Usually they will still be 'thinking' about doing their own thing five years from now. What do you think the most likely outcome will be after the next five years have expired? Probably they will find their salary has increased pro rata during this period and they will have settled into a comfortable rut. The chances are that the moment will have passed and they will never actually start anything.

In fact, they will usually have completely forgotten about telling anyone they were going to start their own business in five years, but, if the idea is still in their head, they might now be saying 'I just need five *more* years'. The initial five years becomes ten; five years since they first 'decided' to start their business and a further period of the same time again. Meanwhile, they're five years closer to their retirement.

If you haven't faced this scenario yourself, then stop and think how many times you have heard others making this statement.

If you work in a large organisation there will always be a few work colleagues who have promised themselves (and their workmates) that they will be leaving to start up their own project. Perhaps you are one of the silent minorities who has resisted boasting about your plans and one day (perhaps even one day soon) you will simply make the break and do it.

If you do, I bet if you were to go back and visit your ex-workmates, once your business is up and running, you would find most of those who were always 'about to start their own business' still sitting in the same old seats, doing the same old jobs. Some may have left to join other companies, others might have retired, one or two may even have died – they call this natural wastage – but you get the picture. The only difference is that they now look five years older. Give them this book.

What about this for a worst case scenario: You start a public relations company but you mess it all up big time; you make every mistake in the book. As a result you go bust in two years flat. You sit down and work out what bits worked and what bits didn't, and you decide to start again. By the time you get to the five-year point you are three years into venture number two and everything is going great guns. Boy, do you learn quickly when you have to! Unless you are really stupid, the chances are that you will have gained from making a hash of things the first time and will know not to repeat your mistakes. As a result your second venture is more likely to succeed.

In fact, it is often preferable to fail first and fail fast than to limp on for years. When the horse is dead it is time to get off. People in business need to think fast and act fast, and you will need to exercise the same ruthlessness and decisiveness in starting business number two as you will in getting the first one off the ground.

Many people, having failed at their first attempt, merely go back to working for somebody else. This can then quickly lead to resentment and a feeling that you are stuck in a job with no future prospects and your career has not really progressed. You might start to feel that you are at the end of the road and this can cause disenchantment, because you know only too well that all of your efforts are going into the pockets of somebody else – your boss! My advice is to accept the possibility of failure and resolve to learn from it: quickly pick yourself up and start all over again.

The key is to remember that there is no substitute for experience. You must never lose sight of this.

You will learn quickly when you deal with the customer experience from start to finish, and you will find ways to improve and do things better by trial and error. You will have to make it work in order for your venture to survive. What better motivator can there be?

Many people make the mistake of starting a business that is little more than an extension of their existing full time job. This may prove to be unsuccessful because being an employee in a particular field does not always mean you can make the transition from employee to business owner. You may have the experience to do your job well while working for somebody else – as a motivated and ambitious person, this is probably not in doubt – but you may lack the acumen to convert these skills into operating your own successful business.

There can be a variety of reasons for this, but the most common one is that most employees are just one of the cogs in the wheel that makes the overall operation revolve. For example, say you now work in manufacturing as a full time job but yearn to start your own manufacturing-based enterprise. Where you currently work you will be part of a team that consists of a sales force, buyers, marketing people, distributors etc. You may only be an expert in the area of actual production, and this alone might take up all of your time when you leave to start your own company.

How then would you set about finding your customers in the first place; and how would you market and distribute the items that you intend to make once you have the customers to sell them to? You need to thoroughly assess the overall picture, not just your individual skill set, before taking the decision to go into the same kind of business, because you could discover that you are out of your depth controlling an entire operation.

By the same virtue, a successful chef working in an established restaurant will usually, at some point or other, decide to open his or her own establishment. What they frequently tend to forget is that they need the expertise of others to make any restaurant a success. The chef will need a sommelier to serve wine, staff to wait on tables, somebody to write the customers' bills and a front of house manager *BEFORE* they open their doors for business. All of these staff cost money and the chef can't do everything themselves because they need to be where they belong – in the kitchen. How then do they move from being a chef for an existing establishment to becoming the owner of their own restaurant? It is not easy. Probably the best way would be to form an alliance with a wine waiter, a front of house manager etc. who can all bring their individual skills to the table (excuse the pun) and manage their own particular parts of the operation. Another way, of course, would be to establish a restaurant as part of a hotel in some kind of business arrangement that might be mutually beneficial. Either way a chef, no matter how brilliant he or she is, must not fall into the trap of thinking that just because they are the master of their kitchen, they would make a natural master of an entire operation.

This is why successful businesses are often formed by people who enter industries that are entirely unrelated to their previous jobs. They take on a start-up venture with little or no experience of that industry, but they still manage to create a level of expertise that is impressive. In fact, Michael Gerber, in his book *The E-Myth*, maintains that most small businesses struggle to grow because people are not entrepreneurs but technicians suffering from an entrepreneurial seizure.

What he means is that when the guy who works as a garage mechanic starts a business that is little more than an extension of his old job, all he continues to do is to fix cars. There is nothing wrong with this of course, other than the fact that he never progresses beyond being a garage mechanic who is self-employed. He fails to concentrate on all the other essential factors that combine to make a business and he never really achieves the level of success that he should. Okay, it is his business so he has dumped the boss, but he won't be able to buy that yacht in Monaco in a hurry. It's important to recognise that leaving your job and working for yourself doing the same thing is not intrinsically entrepreneurial; it is not a business, rather it is self-employment.

However, if you can distil what it is you do, turn it into a process and extend it then this can be a business. In fact many people have made money by expanding upon something they already do well.

For example, I used to own a health club and spa. One of the things we did well was to get new members, so I set up a business generating customers for other gyms. Maybe you are involved in a business that makes widgets and you have a great way to make widgets faster or better or for less. Now, you can become a self-employed widget maker, or you could teach other widget makers your skill or process. Invariably the process is worth far more than the activity.

This is where your competitors can become your best customers. I could make more money generating customers for my competitors using my method than I ever would have if I just stuck to running my own club.

What are you good at? What do you do better than other people? Can you quantify that activity? Can you turn it into a process you can either sell or operate for other people? This can really set you free.

Conversely, when people leave employment to start a business that is totally unrelated to their former job, they are more likely to take the time and trouble to learn a completely new set of skills that incorporates things like sales, marketing, customer service and basic accounting – key skills that are vital components of any successful business.

Consider this: when we are at school we learn and move on; we are always progressing to the next stage, the next year. But when we are in our normal lives we seem to lose sight of the moving on part. Ask yourself how long you would stay in a school year. Would you happily stay at the same level for five years? Absolutely not: so why when we have learnt the process in our adult lives do we not move on? We get lazy in our rut and forget we are supposed to move up a step. A year is a good measure. I personally shake my life up every six months. My birthday is June 1st, conveniently occurring six months into the year, so I have a New Year blitz and a birthday blitz.

Always avoid trading time for money, unless it is someone else's time!

Excuse 5: I Don't Know About Business, Tax or Accountancy

Most of us don't when we get started. But the world is full of information: websites, books, podcasts and any number of seminars, many organised by business associations such as Business Link or the local Chamber of Commerce. They might try to sell you something, but the information is invariably good and I am sure you can resist buying. There is a vast amount of business-related information out there waiting for you to grab and the best bit is that much of it is free. The local Chambers and Business Link will also organise regular networking events and you should make your presence felt at these because they are devised as a cost-effective way of promoting your own business and for finding out what other people are doing.

Most importantly you have already taken the step of picking up this book, demonstrating that you're ready to learn. By the time you finish the final chapter, you will have a three-month plan to get your new business from conception to customer, with lots of tips and useful advice to help you avoid the pitfalls that many only learn too late. I have tried to make this book as complete as possible, and not only show you how to do it but also relate it to my real life experiences and give you a friendly kick up the behind to get you started. Above all, the book will show you that you can learn on your feet while you're standing on them and take a relaxed approach to riding the waves of success and failure. Everything I learned was done in exactly this way and, while it was tough at times, it served me well. Later on I'll be providing explanations of key components of the business start-up process, and each will be easy to implement. There's no reason not to think that taking the plunge might be just around the corner.

And, just as I am guiding you through this book, you could get yourself a mentor. Who do you know who is a pretty successful businessperson? Tell them your idea and they will probably be enthusiastic and want to help. People are always scared that someone will run off with their ideas, but I have always found that entrepreneurs are passionate about business and will freely give advice and information to likeminded people. Nothing can prepare you more than practical experience and it is always better to learn from those who have 'done it themselves'.

Business, tax and accountancy are vast topics, but there is also a wealth of resources available to help fill in any gaps in your knowledge. So don't ignore it – if you don't know it, go and find out.

> '*The greatest glory in living lies not in never failing, but in rising every time we fail*'.
>
> Nelson Mandela

The Lessons to be Gained from this Chapter

- You don't need money to start your business.
- Don't put the cart before the horse: find your customer first – *before* you buy the product.
- Listen rather than talk.

- Walk before you run – don't spend on 'show' before you have the customers to pay for it.
- Contacts that can help you in your business can be better than money.
- Establish your priorities in life before it is too late.
- The world is not against you – you only think it is.
- Become the controller of your own destiny.
- Always embrace failure as a learning experience.
- There is no substitute for knowledge.
- Learn the difference between being 'self-employed' and owning a business.
- Concentrate on doing what you are good at.
- Find yourself a business mentor you can confide in.

CHAPTER 5

THE INVENTION MYTH

*I*nvention is the national lottery of entrepreneurship.

You don't have to re-invent the wheel to make your fortune in business. In fact, new inventions are often the hardest way to achieve success. Building a business around new inventions can often equate to being the national lottery equivalent of entrepreneurship.

Just like the lottery there are the winners that make you want to play, like the Post-it Note and the Rubik's Cube. Who would not be inspired and motivated by the success their inventors have achieved? But the bald facts are that, if you want to make a lot of money the most proven and simplest method is to look at a competitive market and think about how you could do it better. With this in mind, you should be looking towards innovative evolution instead of pure innovation.

You have heard of the cutting edge, right? Well there is also a bleeding edge, and you don't want to be at the bleeding edge of innovation – because for all the creativity and excellence that manifests itself at the edges of new product development, the bleeding edge is just a money pit!

I'll give you a couple of examples. I have set up and run around 20 companies in my life. As I have already said, I got

off to an early start at the age of 12, but during my entrepreneurial career I have had a couple of new-to-market
products that were simply amazing. They would change
the world and couldn't fail – or could they? I found out the
hard way!

I had an exclusive agency to provide polymer lithium ion
batteries in the UK two years before anyone else and we had
everyone from large manufacturers to small producers really
interested. They loved the technology; the batteries were
cheaper, lighter and could be designed in more flexible
shapes than conventional lithium ion batteries. They were
also more stable and environmentally friendly. It was the
technology all manufacturers had been waiting for.

I went to hundreds of meetings and presentations, where
everybody tested samples and agreed that they were amazing
and that they needed to look at getting them into their
products. The letters of intent we received, and the evangeli-
cal conversations from the people we showed them to,
seemed to be a guarantee that the business was a sure fire
hit. But we discovered, to our dismay, that we could never
get traction, just sample orders here and there and no big
bites. Then, about two years later, Panasonic came along with
a very similar product and took the market by storm. Now,
pretty much every portable device uses the technology, from
tablet PCs to mobile phones – and even electric vehicles.
Our technology was right, but, alas, our timing was not, and
we didn't have the funds of Panasonic to keep plugging away
until we broke through.

Another business I tried was selling personal telephone
numbers. This was back in the day when you could not take

your mobile phone number with you; it belonged to the network. So, I would sell a number that you could make ring anywhere you wanted, at home, on your mobile or in the office. The service could even try a few numbers for you and track you down – it really was quite innovative and clever, and you could choose a particular number just like having a personal number plate on your car. This venture was more successful than the batteries but was a really hard slog and I discovered that there was much more money in simply selling mobile phones to the same people, like everyone else.

The biggest challenge was explaining all the benefits of the service to people who were hearing of these solutions for the first time. It wasn't that they weren't impressed, but logistically it was much harder to make a breakthrough. Conversely, the same customers already knew the benefits of a mobile phone, so that simpler, less innovative sale was, in practice, so much easier.

I have seen numerous widgets and gadgets fall by the wayside because the act of selling them was very labour intensive or because small companies, for all their nimbleness, can't match up to the large multinational companies, which see a market and can exploit their reputation and distribution network to put the solution in front of a very large audience very quickly.

I have learnt that it is far easier to try and win a pound someone is already prepared to spend than to try and get them to spend a pound they do not currently spend.

What do I mean? People are more likely to spend their hard-earned cash on something they are familiar with and convinced of the merits of, and less likely to buy an entirely new product, no matter how innovative it may be. A business buyer, by way of example, might see the value of a desk-based gadget that keeps staff cool in a cheaper, more environmentally friendly fashion than an expensive air-conditioning system. But they probably don't have a budget for gadgets, so it stops at the first stage, where the buyer testifies just how wonderful and revolutionary the product is, before committing to the expensive, inefficient air-conditioning system that they're authorised to purchase.

When you are looking for a business, look for something everybody is doing. This sounds counterintuitive but the free market is like nature and nature abhors a vacuum, so if no one is doing it, maybe it's because it won't work. That is not to say nothing will be invested in something new, but it is automatically a lot more work – and I can guarantee that you will fail more times with invention than you will in a crowded market selling apples. If dozens or hundreds of companies are already selling the same or similar products and they are all making a success of it, then you know the product most likely sells. If nobody is interested in a particular item or product then leave it alone, because there is probably something fundamentally wrong with it.

A Lesson about Trying to Launch an Innovative Product in the UK

A company I once dealt with developed some really cool technology for the telecoms market, which limited the effects of radiation from mobile devices on the human body.

Basically, tests on WiFi and mobile devices have shown that there is a physiological reaction in the human body to the radiation these emit, albeit the levels are fairly low. This technology stopped that reaction and, therefore, created an argument that the product made mobile devices safe to use. This was the only such product to have proper laboratory studies to back it up and to have peer group reviews published in scientific journals etc.

The guy who set it up had sold a telecoms company for £46 million and invested about £10 million of that into this business. He employed the best people from the industry, took attractive offices in London and invested heavily in routes to market. However, after just a couple of years I got the 'letter to creditors' through the post; the venture had gone bust.

They had a great product, something that was a technological breakthrough that everyone should use, but they hadn't thought about who would pay for it and how they would get them to. Manufacturers could include it as a part of the phone, but they did not want to add to the cost of the handset. Networks could offer it, but again it would reduce their margin and they would also have to admit they had a possible safety issue.

They also had huge problems with the corporate team they employed. They were used to dealing with large businesses and managing contracts. All of these factors held them back; the technology was clever, but that alone is not enough. In this instance they lost out, and I lost out too.

So maybe there is a further lesson here. Not only should you be careful when starting an 'invention business' but you should be careful when supplying them. It may all sound great, and you will think it is an amazing idea, but stop and think: is this a pound that is already being spent?

One final thing, if your idea *is* an invention, please don't let my book be your excuse for not doing anything. I would hate to stop you before you start; but perhaps consider that it might be wise to introduce the invention as part of a conventional business. So, if it is a replacement to the traditional shoe, try offering it through a shoe shop. I mean this only metaphorically to imply that it may be better to start a shoe shop and sell the invention alongside 'normal' shoes as an alternative. If your idea is great then it will soon take over most of the sales and you will have the right customer in front of you that you can pitch your idea to, with a fall back if they are not one of life's early adopters.

Another way is to start it part time and on a small scale until it is generating good repeat revenues, before going headlong into it. Remember, most technology and innovation companies have massive budgets: the Silicon Valley model of throwing money at it until it works. In this model, mind-boggling figures are key; earning publicity and garnering excitement via Google, Twitter, YouTube and eBay would all be worthless without the persistent, relentless investment that forces them through the innovation barrier and on to stardom. Indeed, there are thousands that have taken tens of millions of pounds of investment and still never quite made it. Unless you're sitting on that kind of capital (and I'd hazard a guess that you aren't), then starting small and concentrating on establishing a steady revenue is almost certainly the way to go.

Differentiation

The key is to understand how to differentiate in a crowded marketplace and then ask why they should buy from you. In my telecoms business I was often asked who my biggest competitor was, and my answer would be 'apathy'. Basically people were not inclined to make a change – you can have a much better offering but getting them away from their existing provider and over the line – securing that sale – is where the challenge starts.

Only great differentiation will break down that apathy. Luckily, there are some great examples of this we can look at.

EasyJet and Southwest Airlines

These operators didn't invent air travel, but they sat down with a blank sheet of paper and really empathised with the customer, and then, importantly, got on with the job. They found a way to revolutionise the airline industry. In fact, there were precedents. Although what Stelios Haji-Ioannou started was pretty revolutionary for this country, Freddie Laker had already achieved as much before, by operating a low cost airline called Skytrain that flew across the Atlantic, on a much smaller scale, back in the 1960s. What Stelios did was to take inspiration from this and adapt the model of the highly successful American company Southwest Airlines, Anglicising it to fit the European market. Southwest's success is fascinating, and its remarkable growth can be explained by its, at the time, revolutionary decision to stick to a single aircraft type (the Boeing 737) in order to stand- ardise maintenance and parts costs. Its founder, Herb

Kelleher, became a legend in the airline industry for taking on the big boys and undercutting them. The company became so successful that in 2003 it was valued higher than all of the other US passenger airlines combined.

Aside from the incredible simplicity of its model, Southwest reached out to customers with an extremely wacky marketing policy, which created a perception that the airline is fun to fly with. It is well worth reading Herb Kelleher's book *Nuts*, which explains how a small regional company grew into a huge mega-carrier and gained enormous respect from its peers as well as the public. A second book, by Jody Hoffer Gittell, called *The Southwest Airlines Way – Using the Power of Relationships to Achieve High Performance* is another business 'bible' that you should read because it discusses how the successful policies employed by the company have managed to generate 10–15% growth for over 31 years.

There is another true story worth telling that illustrates Kelleher's belief that normal business conventions can sometimes be thrown to the wind in order to achieve goals. Kelleher refused to see the wisdom of employing expensive lawyers to litigate over a major route dispute he was having with a rival airline. So, instead of sorting the matter out in a protracted court battle, the two bosses agreed to stage an arm wrestling match in Southwest's hanger in front of an audience gathered from the members of staff from both companies who cheered their bosses enthusiastically. The 'prize' to the winner was the lucrative right to fly on a certain route. Kelleher beat his opponent, dare I say 'hands down'. The rival airline boss conceded that the better man had won on the day and the dispute was ended quickly and without the need for either company to waste vast sums of money on lawyers' fees. Seems sensible to me! Also, what an awesome PR stunt for both parties, as I am sure it was picked up by all the news channels and papers. I love these sorts of guerrilla marketing approaches.

Another great example of this is the famous entrepreneur Michelle Mone, owner of Ultimo, the competitor to Wonderbra, who took a normal bra and made it better. There was already a huge market, with people spending money. All that Ultimo did was to add one tweak – an important one that ensured its product enhanced the appearance of its customers. In order to hammer this message home and differentiate themselves from their competitors, they came up with a novel publicity stunt to get this message across.

They got their product into Selfridges and, on the day of the launch, staged a mock demonstration outside the store with people dressed as doctors and surgeons holding placards calling for a ban on the Ultimo bra, claiming that the bra would put surgeons out of work as women concluded breast enlargement operations were no longer necessary. It sounds crass, but so many people stopped to see what was happening that the police had to close Oxford Street. The television news picked it up and before you knew it there was a huge number of people who had now heard of Ultimo, who knew it made your breasts look bigger and who knew it was sold in Selfridges in London. – can you imagine what that is worth? A simple twist and a clever bit of marketing established the brand as fresh and different. It hasn't looked back.

DVD Rental by Post

This was the work of genius. People were already spending their money on DVD rentals when this model was thought up, but DVD rental by post made it more convenient and, most interestingly, put some trust in the consumer to return disks without threatening them with fines. I love the trust approach to business. There are so many opportunities to excel simply by trusting your customers, yet so many people approach business from the perspective that the world is out to defraud them. Consequently they build their business model in such a way that it frustrates the large majority of honest customers in order to protect against a minority. I always speculate that many companies, by simply trusting their customers instead of doubting their honesty, would more than make up in extra sales the deficit they encountered as a result of any fraud that occurred.

Companies like LOVEFiLM developed a brilliant business model by envisaging a way to tweak an existing business and create tangible benefits for customers. These benefits include not having to go to the video store to browse through titles, no penalty charges for retaining a film too long, free return postage and a flexible system that allows you to view as many films as you want each month all for a single fixed membership fee, providing you return the previous film.

The operation is successful because LOVEFiLM controls the number of films out on hire at any time to one per member, and they leave it to their members to determine when to send back the film they have just watched in order to receive their next one. LOVEFiLM also benefits from revenue from *EVERY* customer, the active and the not so active. The standard video store only benefits when someone comes in and rents a film.

So, this change in the business model that already exists completely alters everything and makes a much bigger, stronger business. You can measure the impact that DVD rental by post had on the industry by counting the number of rental stores in your local high street. They're on the retreat. LOVEFiLM made its service stand out and trounced the competition.

None of these companies re-invented the wheel – in fact my most successful businesses have been in telecoms, IT and the call centre industry, all very cut throat and not at all original. My success in these fields owed less to the products or services I am involved with and more to the way that I approached the industry; it is this that makes the difference.

Now, when I am looking at businesses to invest in or acquire, I always look for simple, competitive industries; the way I describe my criterion is:

I want a business I can describe in a sentence.

As the above examples have demonstrated, the key to cracking a difficult market is not about invention per se, but rather about possessing a key differentiator that makes your product stand out. So, before you do anything, think long and hard about how you will do the same. If you can't describe your product in a simple, easy-to-understand way, you'll struggle to make its value felt by a disinterested public.

Consider what frustrates the customer experience currently, and solve that problem. I describe it as finding and then scratching the itch.

Can you make your service faster, cheaper, more targeted to a group of consumers, easier to buy or more conveniently available?

Go out and ask people who currently buy the product or service that you want to compete with what they would like to see, or what would make them change supplier. How can you break the cycle of apathy and make them care?

The Lessons to be Gained from this Chapter

- Innovation is easier to launch than invention
- PR stunts can provide a low cost way to get your differentiation across
- Find a crowded market – and look at that
- If you really want to launch an invention, perhaps consider launching from within a 'normal' business in the same sector
- Make sure you have a key differentiator

CHAPTER 6

TAKING
RESPONSIBILITY

W*hen you are evaluating the risk of just doing it, why not try thinking of the risk of not doing it?*

Try to imagine yourself in the driving seat of your business and think of all that you might gain; then look back at what you have now. This should put everything in perspective for you. If you think that your life is dull at the moment, then think of all of the opportunities you could have and how your life could change for the better when you start your own business.

Once you have got your ideas together there are a few other things that you must learn to develop.

Your Character versus Your Ego

Character is very important in running a business. I would break this into two main subjects. The first is taking responsibility for your actions and endeavours. The second is ego – and your ability to do things for the right reasons.

Responsibility
Have you ever met one of those people who believe things that happen are everybody's fault but their own? I'm going

to assume that you have, because we are living in a society that has, in recent years and decades, set about systematically abolishing the notion of 'the accident' in favour of making everything someone else's fault. From the person who burns themselves by spilling coffee to the person who trips on a paving slab, there is an impulse to blame the coffee store or the council. This is absurd – accidents happen. I might even venture so far as to suggest that the individuals might not have been paying attention to what they were doing. But we prefer to assume others are at fault rather than concede that we can be clumsy or inattentive.

Meanwhile, litigation culture is spreading to this country fast, chiefly from America. You will have seen the advertisements on television that encourage you to contact this or that company if you have fallen over at work, contracted a bug after eating a take away meal or difficult surgery has gone wrong. Accidents can never be completely eradicated; sometimes people do get hurt and sometimes it happens by accident not because somebody has been negligent. As I have already mentioned, life is a risk; but I am afraid that a blame culture is spreading and has given birth to a completely new kind of industry that is not particularly wholesome.

The problem with this attitude is that people live in a cosy bubble of diminished responsibility. They take their pay home, but if the company fails it is someone else's fault. If they crash their car, the insurance company pays up. There are no life lessons.

This is probably why people find bereavement so hard, because more often than not there is no one to blame, and we must face the fact that sometimes things happen for no reason. The more the blame culture spreads, the more we as a society will struggle with grief and our failure to rationalise something so completely counterintuitive.

So how does this work in business? Well, you can only learn a lesson when you accept the true cause. If you ask people why their business failed, or perhaps why a marketing campaign failed, some of the answers they give are truly insightful – for all the wrong reasons. You'll hear everything from the economic downturn to fraud and theft, the vagaries of the fickle market they are targeting and so on. The real reason is, with some truly unfortunate exceptions, that they got it wrong; they failed – not always because of personal fault, but invariably as a consequence of their own actions. Accepting the truth of that is a good thing, because as soon as we can accept that and progress beyond just paying lip service to our failings, we can really see how we failed and discover how to avoid the same pitfalls the next time around.

If they believed the economy was against them, why is it that every company in their market didn't go bust? Why did some survive and others thrive and grow in the same conditions? When this occurs I think the failures are merely looking for a scapegoat by blaming everyone and everything but them-selves. But people do this, in part, because for some reason our society has come to view failure as something derogatory, when in fact this is not so.

It can happen because people haven't shown sufficient fore-sight or they have failed to act in accordance with a changing set of circumstances. It can happen because they failed to spot the weather turning. But, whatever the cause is, the entrepreneur ultimately must find fault with him or herself, rather than other people. Although most businesses that fail do so in the formative years, this isn't always the case. Others that may have been successful over longer periods can also fail and this can be for a variety of reasons that usually reflect on the marketing policies of the company or failure to detect that a demand no longer exists for their products.

When you are involved in a business you have to ensure that you keep your finger on the pulse and become constantly aware of any changes in the market that are likely to affect what you do. Essentially you will need to learn to change with the times. Steve Jobs and Apple spotted a wonderful opportunity with mp3 players and their genius design and marketing ensured that the iPod comprehensively took over from the personal CD player. However, this did not happen overnight and there are usually plenty of early warning signs that things are set to change.

The Italians have a phrase that states: 'the fish stinks from the head down'. In other words, problems can all be traced to the top. Learn to stand up and say 'I was wrong; I cocked it up'. Once you can say that with absolute confidence you can move on and up quickly.

What people say and what they really mean are often not the same thing. For example:

'Our customers did not pay us on time'.
In reality what this means is you didn't collect the money from your customers on time and failed to chase them sufficiently. This is called bad credit control.

'The economy or my market changed'.

What this means is that you failed to adapt when the market was moving around you and that you failed to keep your finger on the pulse and be alert to any changes.

'We were sued and had to close down'.

The real issue is that, because you had inadequate protection in place, you left yourself vulnerable.

'We ran out of money'.

This can happen when you do not sell enough of your product or services (this explanation underlies most excuses).

'A supermarket opened down the road and killed off our business'.

This can happen to the best of us, but you saw it being built for a year and did nothing effective to react to the situation.

So now you have accepted that the problem is you, you can start again with the clear idea of what went wrong and learn from it. If only people embraced this more in life we would be in a happier society.

Ego – Doing Things for the Right Reason

Having a grand vision is a must. I believe you should set out with a big idea and a big vision of where you are going to take it. Where I think it potentially all goes wrong is when you create a fabrication for your staff and customers, something that departs from reality in order to impress, and you fall into the dangerous trap of starting to believe your own rubbish. Huge egos can be extremely dangerous – especially when you fail to deliver what your customers expect of you. It is far better to be humble and likeable.

Following are two examples where, for the protection of the egos concerned, we will change the names.

Company A

Company A went into a business that was typically a low margin, high revenue business in the outsourcing industry. The person who set it up came from a corporate background and was targeting blue chip customers. The problem was that ego got in the way of the commercial part. Firstly, they had very expensive – and I mean *very* expensive – offices that were totally unnecessary for an outsourced operation. This alone was business suicide.

Secondly, their overwhelming desire to deal with the most admired blue chip companies was so great that they took on loss-making work just to enable them to say 'Look who we work for', flaunting their flagship customers to others.

Unsurprisingly, the business went bust. I got involved in rescuing it and, by applying some sound common sense business principles, reduced its overheads, got rid of the loss-making clients and helped the company to make a strong profit over the next few months. We didn't, however, change the management, and a powerful definition of insanity is to carry on doing the same thing and expect a different result.

In retrospect, it was a foregone conclusion that it wouldn't last. The employees were still living in an imaginary world, seeing the turnaround as a sign that things would keep getting better. New people joined and a new pool table was installed so that the staff could enjoy their leisure time. Is it surprising that they went bust again and I lost a pile of money (my fault)? They are now miraculously on their third incarnation and you know what? They have lovely offices and a big blue chip customer that loses them money.

Company B

Company B was in the sustainable clothing market. They spent £500,000 very quickly, trying to expand as fast as possible. They devoted their time and resources to getting very expensive worldwide patents on their brand names, and duly won the growing business award for best new product. Before long they managed to get their clothing into the best department stores.

Sounds great doesn't it? However, when you looked under the surface it was swiftly apparent that the reason they were in the top department stores was that they had concluded a commercially insane deal where they kept the stock and let the customer draw down without being committed to a minimum order. This was done on 30 day credit terms, so they had to sit on tons of stock that they had already paid for, with below market average margins. It was all for ego, image and presentation. Their clothes were seen and sold in upmarket locations, but the business plan was built on glaring fault lines. Not only this, but the stores called all the shots. When reality kicked in, it turned out they were selling pitiful numbers of items, below even their own most pessimistic prediction.

As I've indicated previously, sometimes you lose out making a business deal, but this was one occasion where I got away unscathed. I looked hard at doing a rescue deal with them, but the guy remained so deluded – motivated by his own ego and his conviction that his business was the market leader – that I decided to leave well alone. Until the company admits that its marketing policy is suicidal, it'll keep failing.

I found another company which produces almost identical items to them, even to the point of having a similar logo (but not enough to infringe their £70,000 worth of protection), and they are in every major and minor shop in the country. This business is growing like crazy and yet it set up at roughly the same time. So, while the guy at Company B was intent on building his ego and his empire, his competitor was out there getting his hands dirty.

I am guilty of not being entirely innocent. I have seen the traits in these examples in myself over the years and I can assure you that it is tempting and easy to fall into the trap. I can be sure of what I am saying because it echoes tales of actors who believe in their own publicity; well, this is equally true of those of us who run a business. In political circles it is known as 'spin'. When you run your own business you never want to take steps backwards. The secret is being aware of your own fallibilities and ensuring that you take steps to prevent your ego from taking the upper hand.

If you have taken a wrong turn it is a damn sight easier to reverse up and go the right way than to stay on the wrong road and see if you can find your way later on. Remember you are doing this for yourself not for anyone else; make your decisions quickly and act upon them, don't be the bunny in the headlights or the prisoner of your own inflated ego.

Action is the differentiator in life; knowledge is nothing without action.

The Lessons to be Gained from this Chapter

- It is better to set up a business that sells a well tried and tested product than something that is unknown or is a new invention.

- Be customer driven – you should always think in terms of your customer being right, even when they aren't.

- Weigh up the pros and cons of starting a business in your chosen industry.

- Plan your business, but do not over-plan so that it stands in the way of your productivity or finding your first customers.

- Knowledge in itself is not enough – you need to make use of what you learn.

- Become involved in networking at every opportunity because this will provide the opportunity of learning from your peers.

- Develop your character – *NOT* your ego.

- Never blame others for the mistakes that you make.

- Keep your finger on the pulse at all times so that you can detect changes in your industry and markets before it is too late.

- Believe in your abilities – *NOT* in your own 'spin'.

CHAPTER 7

THE FOUR
STAGES OF
ENTERPRISE

The next chapters of this book are all about action. I hope you've realised by now that I don't want you to finish this book, briefly muse on its contents, put it back on the shelf and carry on dreaming. I want you to take positive steps forward and really and truly get started.

So, as you progress through the next three chapters, I will pepper them with actions and tasks. Put the book down and do these actions, then come back and carry on.

The first thing I am going to tell you, you may find a little discouraging. You should not start a big business as your first business. It may *become* big, but there is a right of passage that will serve you well, and people who shortcut it miss important early lessons that they then have to learn later, when there is a lot more at stake. Ask almost any business owner and what most of them will agree, if they are being honest, is that they are amazed how many of the logical things that should have worked did not. It is truly incredible how logic defying business can be, and until you have really felt it a few times, nothing can prepare you for it, or the pressure it can put you under. So, far better to experience this pressure and these challenges when it is only you and you are just starting to grow, than later when you have more to lose and carry the responsibility of others on board.

The day that I thought I knew the most about business was the day I started. Every year since then I have realised how much more there is to experience and understand. I reckon I know about 10% of what there is to know, and fortunately for me that is 9.5% above average.

Bearing the above in mind, you need to be careful with advice. Everyone is an advisor, but very few are advising from experience. Their arguments may be well intentioned and sound, from a logical viewpoint, but, as I have already mentioned, logic is no guarantor of success. The problem with advice like this is that you tend to listen to the best debater, the person who is most adept at getting their particular point of view across. If no one has any direct experience of what you are doing, then you may as well follow your intuition and make your own decisions. Be clear if asking for advice and above all else see if they have direct experience in this field. Even then, don't feel obligated to follow the advice you get.

If you said that you were looking to market a product aimed at the over 55 single male market, conventional wisdom would tell you to list a number of logical routes, such as advertising in pubs, each of which you can guarantee will have single men over 55 present, or forming an alliance with SAGA, who are experts at hitting that target market. All borne out of logic, and not bad advice. However, try approaching people with 'has anyone ever marketed a product aimed at the over 55 single male market?' You will quickly find out if anyone has anything other than ideas to add to the mix. I am not diminishing the value of ideas, but experience wins hands down.

In discouraging you from starting a big business, please don't think I am saying you should not think big – of course you should. But what I am driving at is: begin small, with your target market very clearly defined, gain experience for yourself, talk to people with direct know-how and make something scalable.

If you want to build strong foundations and be able to grow your business in a sustainable and safe manner, you need to go through four stages of enterprise. I have not separated these by turnover or number of employees, like many people try and do. Instead, far more importantly, I've separated them by knowledge and experience. When you have grown out of each stage you move to the next, reinforcing the importance of continuous learning and development. Remember, nothing prepares you for the reality of running your own business like the process of doing so – and doing so thoroughly, not rushing to the next plateau.

By far the most important benefit of going through these stages in the correct order, only advancing to the next once you have mastered the previous, is that doing so will ensure you will have more money, more stability and less stress. The stress, anxiety and cash flow problems that many business owners go through are caused by their running on ahead, scaling up before they are ready and suffering from being ill prepared. It's happened to so many business owners and it's happened to me, so I am speaking from experience. Follow the four stages.

1. Out on Your Own

This is you when you're just getting started. It's the point in the process when it is just you and your customers, when you will learn how to perform the following vital business tasks.

Selling

This is an essential skill and you will learn a lot when you sell your own product. If you are new to sales, there are lots of books on the subject, don't dismiss it as something you don't do. Challenge yourself, you did not give up walking just because you fell flat on your face, so if this is your weakest area, challenge yourself, overcome it. You don't have to behave like a polished estate agent type to sell; sales is often as much about passion and sincerity as clever language and closes. Be confident in yourself and your product and just be yourself, but do please make sure that, after you have explained what you are offering, you ask for the order! Don't bottle it at the last minute. Remember if you cannot sell what you have on offer, it will be very, very hard to get someone else to, and it is an easy trap to fall into to believe that a better salesperson will make the business viable. Instead re-evaluate the product and the offering. People should buy it in viable quantities from whoever is selling it.

Marketing

Marketing is different to sales; one way to look at it is: if you have a room full of people, marketing gets people to put their hands up, sales gets them to place an order. Now marketing can be a strange beast, and you will need to experiment and

GO DO!

test to ensure you can get people to put their hands up cost effectively. It is better to go through this learning curve early when you are out on your own, than to run into problems later on in the business's development. You will find more advice on marketing in Chapter 10.

Buying
When I had my market trading business, there was an expression 'bought right is half sold'. Never accept that the price is the price when dealing with suppliers, always be looking around, and always review your suppliers. Loyalty is important but margin is *massively* important to your survival, so make sure you are always buying right. Countless numbers of businesses get off to a bad start because they don't know how to negotiate and buy.

Dealing with Customers
I always joke that business would be great if you did not have staff and customers. You will have some lovely customers, but you will have your share of difficult, illogical and crazy ones too. Therefore, you need to understand the challenges you're likely to face with customers before you move beyond being your own boss. It is much better that you get a solid feel for what is expected of you and what works. You should also be looking for systems which will make customer service easier; so if a customer does x, we do y. This can be the foundation of a customer service manual that will be invaluable later on. I hate it when I call a company because of a problem and have to argue for ages with lots of different people to get some compensation. If they had a proper manual they could have said, okay sorry about your

problem, I am authorised to give you 'this' and then I, as a customer, would feel it had been dealt with efficiently and that I did not have to scream and get hot under the collar to achieve it.

Basic Bookkeeping

Stop it. I know what you are thinking, and I'm sorry but I really believe you have to do it, just a little bit, yourself, and start to really understand your numbers. Learning to read accounts is not much fun, but the financials are absolutely key to a business's growth and survival – and all too often I am amazed how many people just bury their head in the sand and say 'oh I am just no good at that sort of thing'. If you want to start a business and make a success of it, you need to get good. It is not hard, it is just daunting.

Read some books, get a bookkeeper to explain a P&L and balance sheet to you, go on a short course or seminar and, honestly, if you do not have a grasp of this stuff then you are missing 80% of the picture. Once you get it, you can employ a bookkeeper to do it, but don't stay in the dark completely.

Time Management

You might think you are a multi tasking god, but when you start to run a business you will really discover what a full plate looks like! You need to learn how to use your time efficiently so that you can properly delegate and manage people in the future. There are lots of great books on the subject, but much of it will come naturally as you work out systems to enable you to finish work before 3am every day!

I always remark that entrepreneurs work half days (that is 12 hours every day), but with good time management you can get that down quite a bit.

Managing Cash Flow

This is the big lesson, and please don't employ people to do it for you! There is nothing as harrowing or irresponsible as not being able to pay your payroll. So learn how to manage your cash. Remember that business is all about more money in than out, so as well as being profitable you need to make sure you have good terms from your suppliers and terrible terms for your customers (tongue firmly in cheek). But, seriously, you need to get paid quickly, and you need to pay slowly, you need to keep your short-term forecast up to date and you need to manage your bank account ruthlessly.

Be in Business and Follow These Steps

Like I said, this stage of your business is a right of passage – skip this bit and you will have to learn some very tough lessons later on. You will have higher overheads, you will burn more cash and it will prove very difficult. When you are happy you have learnt the lessons above, and only then, you can move on. But skip this stage at your peril!

2. Small Team – Partners or Employees

This stage is a natural progression from working on your own, and could be either a different business to stage 1 or a growth or continuation of it. If you have run your own business before as a 'one man band' and you feel you have learnt the lessons above, then you can start here, but only if you are sure you can get the marketing, sales and cash flow management right, before you start to employ people. Then, finally, you can begin to grow beyond just you.

This could take the form of partnering with businesses that deliver sales, marketing or other areas, or it could be delegating some of what you do. Obviously it's vital as you scale up that you keep an eye on cash, and ask yourself at every turn whether you could afford your staff even if they brought no added value. Don't employ on the basis that the extra revenue they bring in will pay them, as it might not happen or may take longer than anticipated to get there. The business with just you in it should be generating sufficient extra cash to support this new person.

Until now you have been doing all of these tasks yourself, so it is really important that any new person has a very clear mandate, a job description. They should know exactly what to do, they should know what success and failure look like, and they should have a template from your experience setting out exactly how to do it and what results you have achieved.

They should also be paid well and given lots of training and coaching to get the desired results. Don't expect common sense, don't expect them to work things out themselves, people fear making mistakes and get paralysis if they don't have very clear instructions. The reason you did the 'out on your own' section was so that you could understand the different job functions and, therefore, effectively delegate.

Employees are happiest when they have a very clearly defined and laid out mandate. In other words they know exactly what is expected of them and they know exactly what to do; they don't want to take risks or use initiative for fear of failing. Remember this is why you are different, because you have a different version of what failure is in your mind – don't you?

3. Extended Team – Small Enterprise

Once you get to this stage – and it will be some time after implementing the lessons learned in this book – you will be transitioning your role to one where you develop the business at a strategic, rather than operational, level. Your goal here is to absolve yourself of any day-to-day operational tasks, and simply manage the managers, using the same clear expectations as set out in stage 2.

Most of your time now should be spent looking for partnerships, joint ventures, acquisitions and mergers. You should be looking at new channels to market, at overseas licensing, franchising, taking on investment or spin-off companies. This is the time when the business will really grow, you just need to understand how to get out of the way and help it at a different level.

4. Multiple Teams

This is where you now have in place joint ventures, partnerships and spin-off businesses. You have now been through the full learning curve and, as such, have a castle built on solid foundations of knowledge, experience and organic steady profitable growth, not a house of cards. Remember, if you get here too quickly you will have missed vital business lessons and you should not be surprised to find things tumbling down around you, causing you to face the long, hard slog of starting again from scratch. As I've indicated, you should be prepared for failure and resolved that you won't let it stop you. But be warned: when you fall from this height it is a hell of a fall! Far better getting your mistakes in early. Getting to stages 3 or 4 too quickly is asking for trouble.

Are you clear on the stages and on your priorities in the short term? Okay. Now we get into actually taking you from thought to action.

From now on the only sitting on your behind you should be doing is reading this book.

The Lessons to be Gained from this Chapter

- Don't start a big business as your first business.
- Start small and make something scalable.
- Learn the hard lessons before you employ others.
- Be careful whose advice you take.
- Talk to people with direct know-how and experience.
- Follow the Four Stages of Enterprise in the right order. Many businesses fail by rushing ahead. Don't make the same mistake.
- Master the basics first: buying and selling, marketing, dealing with customers, managing your books, time and cash flow.

CHAPTER 8

PLANNING

I am not a big planner. I like to act and then adapt and change based on feedback, but I am aware that for people who struggle to take action, the way that they plan a business can help them make that leap. So, to encourage you to act, we are going to do some planning.

Fail to Plan and You Plan to Fail

You need to weigh up the pros, the cons, the challenges that you may face and the opportunities that lie ahead of you.

Beware that planning can often be used as an excuse not to act; another thing to put in the way of the real work. This can be a major barrier to action, so you should avoid making excuses to delay taking action, as I have been trying to emphasise throughout the book so far.

Many potential business starters I meet and speak to often have analysis paralysis and end up stuck in the planning stage indefinitely.

This is generally known as 'thinking time' in the trade. Don't get stuck in the same trap; too much time thinking and planning will soon eat into your valuable time; time that you could be using much more productively to put money into your pockets. You obviously need to do a certain amount of planning, but there is often a tendency to over-plan or be too elaborate. You should not let this overshadow the key issue of finding your first customers.

To begin, let's start with an activity.

ACTIVITY: Identifying Personal Weaknesses

I want you to get a pad and paper and write a list of the five weaknesses that you feel are most evident in your skill set. Is it the thought of selling that most intimidates you? Or marketing? You wouldn't be the only one to confess to a weakness with bookkeeping or accounts. Or you might feel that your biggest weakness is an uncertain knowledge of the industry you are targeting. Stop at five areas, and quickly mark them according to their urgency. Now make a quick list of resources that you could use to fill in those gaps – and make sure you put expensive training courses last. Can you devote a bit of time to reading up on the web? Are there books on the topic? Do you know people who have the information you need?

I am not suggesting you go out and get a qualification, or indeed fill in all those gaps right away – but it's important to have a realistic idea of the areas in which you need to improve and to be resolved to address these, bit by bit, as you go. Never become complacent and assume that delaying your learning, or outsourcing the activity, will serve you as well as putting in time as you go along. One day you will be employing someone to do this stuff, but you should still understand it yourself first.

As you acquire this knowledge, you'll swiftly discover that one of the most productive resources is other people who run their own business. These are the best people to ask for advice on the nitty-gritty bits. Buy them a drink and pick their brains, you will be amazed how open entrepreneurs are to talking about their business and their challenges. I will be surprised if you don't know anyone who you could approach for unbiased advice, but if you really can't think of anyone then perhaps look towards your local Chamber of Commerce. I have already mentioned just how valuable their networking events can be because they will provide you with the opportunities to start chatting to established businesspeople. Do not be afraid to share your idea and be as open as possible. You can also look at the many independent networking groups that exist both online and offline. In the UK there are physical networking groups like BNI, NRG Networks and many more – just type business networking and the name of your nearest big town into your search engine.

Online there are also many great resources. Join Ecademy; start reading the blogs and leave comments; ask questions. I have seen some really detailed correspondence start to form, and involvement such as this is a great way to test acceptance of your ideas. When you are ready, start your own blog that is relevant to your sector, but not a pitch for your product, and you will pick up readers and develop a network of people who know you for what you do. It is very easy to take these online contacts offline and meet up for a coffee and a chat. This can lead to hugely beneficial exchanges of ideas and information.

You know that every journey starts with a single step, but even more than that you just need to make sure you keep some forward momentum every day. So, I want to look at some planning that also takes you forward; that gives you your first steps.

ACTIVITY: Making Time

The first step in starting a business is very simple indeed, although not always easy. It involves making time. Clearly everyone is different – some of you will be working full time, some of you will not; some will have a business idea that can easily be run part time, others will need to throw themselves head long into it. So the extent to which you can create time will vary, but the key is making a shift from a position of not acting to a position of doing something every day to keep forward momentum.

Something that works for me is blocking out time, so if you have two hours a day free, put it in your diary that the time is reserved. Do you keep a diary? If not, start; you are about to get very busy and you need to organise your time and your meetings simply and efficiently, so it needs to be something you see and work with every day.

Are you struggling to find two-hour slots? Many people have young families or people to care for, so finding time isn't always easy, but work to identify times you can devote to your business and be disciplined about following through. Even in my busiest times, if I have wanted something enough, I have found ways to make the time without shirking other responsibilities, and it's absolutely vital if you want to make this work. If you've not done so already, this might be a good time to put the TV on eBay.

Now, do you have your first time slot booked? The following action point is not something you need do right now but as soon as that slot becomes available: it's your first step.

ACTIVITY: Make a List of All the Things You Need to Do to Get Going

That sounds like a massive ask, but I'm not asking for detail. Instead, start brainstorming and marking down the things that you need to do. Don't worry about what order to put the items in yet, just think laterally about all the little things that need to be done in order to get started. If you are struggling to come up with this list then try framing it in slightly different terms. Take your piece of paper and write at the top the question 'could I sell my product/service tomorrow?' The answer is presumably no; so ask yourself 'why?' This will help engage your brain differently, as you are answering a question rather than just trying to think of a list. For example, you might say:

Why? Because I need a limited company

Why? Because I need a bank account

Why? Because I need a website

Why? Because I need business cards

Why? Because I need a product

Read the list back. What started as a negative list of things you *don't* have has become a pro-active list of things you need to get. Once your planning is complete, you can begin to work through these tasks.

ACTIVITY: Prioritise Your Tasks

Not all of the items on your list are actionable right now, but you need to start prioritising them and working out which ones need to be addressed first, and with the most urgency. This will make your working time more productive.

The following system I have borrowed from Steven Covey – another author whose books you should read.

Take your list of tasks and begin sorting through it. Each item should be distributed into one of the following categories, turning your one long list into four rather less intimidating sequences of things to do.

List 1 – Urgent and important

List 2 – Urgent but not important

List 3 – Important not urgent

List 4 – Not important and not urgent

List 1 should contain things that without doing you literally cannot move any further forward, like finding a product, finding a customer, buying a mobile phone, setting up the limited company, opening a bank account, that sort of stuff.

List 2 should contain stuff that needs to happen urgently but is not absolutely essential to getting started, like setting up the website, product and pricing of everything.

List 3 includes things that need to be done but can wait – thinking of a name, writing a business plan, doing cash flow forecast – all important, but not before the other things are done.

List 4 is like-to-haves – so this might be a list of things that, while important, can probably be done once you've launched. Examples might include getting brochures printed, branding on the company car or having a launch party.

What you consider should go in each of these sections is, of course, subjective and you may well put things in a different order to me. However, the key is to get your tasks listed and then start to execute your list in strict order. It is all too easy and tempting to jump around and do the easy things first or the bits you feel comfortable and competent about. So this list forces you to take an ordered and time efficient approach to getting started.

Now try putting a time limit on each section, limiting how much time you will spend in each area. When you have timings and an order, put these into your calendar in the two-hour windows you've been diarising, so that you have clear dates, clear deadlines and clear outcomes for each chunk of time.

If you are really time poor, look at what you can do while driving or while on a train or plane. Can you take some time off work and cram it all in that window of opportunity? Can you delegate certain tasks from your list to a family member or business partner? If you want it enough you will find the time!

Once you've created the time and started mapping out what you'll do with it, you can move on to the really exciting stuff.

ACTIVITY: Define Your Product and Your Market
Having read this far, you should have a pretty good idea of what product or service it is you're looking to sell, as well as

knowing at which market it is directed. If not, now is the time to start thinking about what you'll be selling, and to whom.

As we've already discussed, think about your customer first. Who is he or she? Now is not the time to be vague, but to really tailor it down to specifics.

Resist the temptation to generalise. Instead of saying 'anyone with a lorry is a suitable user of our product', you might want to focus on haulage companies with between five and 50 lorries based in the south west of England, for example. Or instead of 'women', it might be women between the ages of 18 and 25 who live inside the M25. By being more specific, it is easier to target your audience.

How big is your market? How many potential customers are there that you can realistically target? Can you find out how much they generally spend on the product or service that you intend to make a success of? If you capture a fraction of that market can it work?

Start thinking about whether you have direct access to these customers through your immediate friends, family and network, and make sure you take the opportunity to talk to them about the product or service, to assess whether they would buy from you and whether they like your unique differentiator.

This element is absolutely key and vital for your business to succeed. You might think your product and your solution is amazing – your mum might say it is amazing too – but find out what the customer thinks first and foremost. Do they see it as adding value, or are they really nonplussed about the proposition? Please try not to load the question in your favour. We all know how to get the answer we want, but that is completely counterproductive.

If anything, take the trouble to reverse the question, finding out what the customer really wants and needs. Instead of asking 'You would buy your widgets from somewhere that delivered much quicker, wouldn't you?' try asking a more important question, such as 'Does it really make any difference if widgets come same day or next day?' This one is slightly weighted towards no, so if the answer is 'Oh yes, it would be life changing' then you know you are onto a winner and not up against apathy.

Remember, you may find your business idea interesting and exciting, but your customer may just see it as a necessary evil and have too much else on their plate to really share your enthusiasm. Spend time on this, and don't stop until you really get a feel for what the customer wants. Only when you know exactly what it is they do want can you properly define your product.

How will you go about delivering on the promise you've made? If you're anything like me, you may even have made a sale without a product on your shelf; and, if so, you have some urgent questions to answer.

Do you know where you will get your product from? This is a vital question; the last thing you want to do is source a product that costs you too much money or takes too long to replenish when stock is exhausted. Have you explored all the possible suppliers, making sure that they can offer exactly what you want, when you need it, at a price that makes good sense?

Do you know how it will be delivered?

If it is a service, is it you that will deliver it or will delivery be subcontracted?

Finally, make sure that you can describe the product in a simple, immediate fashion, in a way that explains immediately what it is you're offering, who will want it and how it will stand out from the competition and solve a real problem.

When you meet people or talk to them, you really need to be able to concisely articulate what it is you have to offer, whether you are looking for a customer and supplier or a new channel or route to market.

You may have heard the expression 'elevator pitch' – born out of the idea that you get into an elevator with Bill Gates (or any other wealthy and influential person) and you have the duration of the elevator ride to pitch him your idea.

This pitch is also a really important cornerstone of the business. As you grow, this is what all new employees and stakeholders need to learn verbatim. They need to be able to recite it to their friends, customers and colleagues. Everyone needs to be a walking, talking advert for your business and they can only do that if you are really clear about your proposition.

Your pitch needs to include:

What you do – Avoid industry terminology and technical information: focus on benefits rather than just features.

Why you do it – A strong why is more engaging with the customer, it is like your mission or quest in life: better if it is not just about the money.

What is unique about what you do – Your USP (unique selling point) or key differentiator: why should they buy from you and not your competitors? You need to give them a compelling reason to use you.

What you are looking for, or what your ideal customer looks like – Many people miss this out, and just give an interesting pitch, with no outcome. What do you need most? Partners, joint ventures, customers, investors? If you don't ask, you don't get. If you tell someone specifically what you are looking for, you will engage their brain in the search. Be specific, not general, so don't say any customer, describe the customer: for example, I am looking for fish and chip shops in the Bournemouth area.

Write your pitch, and say it again and again until it trips off your tongue with clarity and without hesitation.

ACTIVITY: Getting Your Prices and Dealing with Numbers

Anyone who's set up and run a business will tell you that one of the most common schoolboy errors is failing to have a high enough profit margin. Not having enough margin makes running a business a real uphill struggle, and that's one of the reasons that I love service businesses – you can usually get much better margins.

What is a good margin? Well of course it depends on the industry and the demand for the product, which impact upon how much it costs you to find the customer.

A good way to start is to approach your competitors. Make a list of the companies you'll be up against and pick up the phone. Call them all to get accurate costings for their product or service. Once you have a list of prices, work out what it would cost you to deliver the same service or products, and see what the difference is.

Now look at price variation. Is there a big difference in price? Why? What do the more expensive ones do for the extra money? Go to Companies House, which stores all company accounts as a matter of public record, and for a small fee you can download copies of competitors' accounts. Search them and look at how much these organisations turnover and what their gross profitability is like. Don't get too hung up on the comparisons, but try to get a feel for how others are doing. You'll need to be confident you can take them on head on.

Now, how do they get customers? Salespeople? Advertising? Work out how much it will cost you to market the product and how many you'd have to sell to break even. You would be amazed how many people overlook this and end up with products it is impossible to make money from, because it costs as much to get them to the customer as would be made from supplying them.

Only when you have taken all these factors into consideration can you realistically decide on your price, taking into account the competition and your own overheads to make sure that you can both make money and attract customers. The first decision is whether your product or service is premium or cheap. It is always tempting to undercut competition, but you can often be more successful if you can sell less at a premium price.

This is going to be closely related to the appeal of your product and the effectiveness of your key differentiator. If your product really stands out, you'll be able to get away with premium pricing far more easily, as people will buy on the basis of the differentiator, not necessarily the price.

ACTIVITY: List All the Possible Sales Channels that Work for Your Product or Service

Your target customer has been defined, now you need to think about your routes to market. How will you reach that first customer, and how will you find the ones who'll come afterward? How can you be as sure as possible that customers will find you, not your competitors? Luckily, there are many routes to market, or channels, so you have a great many options. Here are some of the key ones that you'll need to consider:

- Shop – High overhead, but a method of getting your products to people
- Concession or stall – A stall or small area in a shop, in a shopping centre or at an event, like a fair or conference
- Retailers – Other people's shops, big or small
- Internet shop – Lower overhead and rapidly taking over from the high street, Christmas sales on the internet in 2010 in the UK exceeded high street sales for the first time (I don't think we will ever look back)
- Internet retailers – Can online shops, like Amazon etc., stock your product?
- eBay – For physical products eBay stores are a great way of immediately opening up to a wide audience

- Telesales – Can you ring people and sell your product or service? Why don't you try? Spend a day on the phone and call prospective customers; see how positive or otherwise the conversations are. If you get a customer from it but hate it, it may be worth exploring how you can delegate it (but please do it yourself first, or you will waste a lot of money on outside agencies)

- Agents – People who sell your product for a commission; this can be via their company, party planning, direct sales or any number of methods

- Email marketing – Sending targeted emails to a list of opted-in potential customers, but don't spam (usually sending them to a squeeze page to capture their information so you can work on them later)

- Joint venture – Email marketing, where you agree to work with someone who has a large database to sell to their customers

- Door to door – Going to company premises or residential houses to offer goods or services

- White label – Offering your goods or services to companies who service your type of client and want to offer your product as their own

- Franchise – Where someone sets themselves up in their own business but follows your rules, uses your name and sells your products and services and you just take a cut (this can be a great way to expand, and made McDonald's and Subway into the world's two largest fast food retailers)

- Direct mail – Where you send people sales letters; this is very effective but can be quite expensive and you need an expert in the area to really make it work

So, which of these could work for you? Some of them? All of them? Try and be really open minded; don't dismiss anything out of hand, as you simply do not know until you try what customer reactions will be.

ACTIVITY: Complete a SWOT Analysis or Ben Franklin Balance Sheet

Finally, it is good to articulate in writing the good and bad things about your idea. It is too easy to get caught up with your own propaganda and not fully evaluate the negatives with the positives. This exercise gives you an opportunity to have a think about the strengths and weaknesses of your business idea.

The Ben Franklin balance sheet is simply the process of taking a sheet of paper, dividing it into two and writing all the good things on one side and the bad things on the other. It is a great way of getting thoughts on paper. However, this can be slightly corrupted by human nature, as you will tend to get the outcome you are looking for! The human brain is clever like that. So if you think it is a good idea you will come up with a million reasons why that is so, with very few drawbacks.

One way round this is to do the SWOT analysis. This makes you think around the business a bit more clearly.

So, with this one, take your piece of paper and write the following headings:

Strengths
Weaknesses

Opportunities

Threats

Then start to populate these headings.

Strengths are things that put you ahead of your competitors; for example, we can offer a friendly local service or we deliver quicker: all the things that make your business strong.

Weaknesses could be that low capital reserves mean you can't out spend competitors on marketing, or it could be that you can't buy stock as cheap as the larger players, that sort of thing.

Opportunities could be that you are involved in talks to be the sole supplier of widgets to schools in the south east, or you can create the only online supplier of x,y,z.

Threats could be a change in legislation, not being able to sell the first order of stock etc. or strong competitors coming into the market.

It is then easy to look at all the factors and assess whether there are holes in your plan, i.e. are the threats very real and the opportunities very tentative, how likely are each of the positives and negatives?

I know the answer you want, and I hope you get it – if not, it simply means you need to go back through your plan and think about finding solutions to those problems. Once you've done that, we're going to spend a bit of time talking about how you go about communicating those solutions to the world at large.

The Lessons to be Gained from this Chapter

- Fail to plan and you plan to fail.
- Identify your weaknesses and focus ruthlessly on improving in these areas.
- Become the master of your time. Put time aside to make sure you get things done.
- Brainstorm to work out what needs doing, and learn to prioritise your tasks.
- Know your market; know your product.
- Develop a pitch and deliver it with confidence and assurance.
- Compare your business to your competitors and learn from them.
- Identify your channels.
- Complete a SWOT analysis or Ben Franklin balance sheet to really get a handle on your business proposition.

Chapter 9

MARKETING

Don't Start a Business, Start a Marketing Campaign

Don't panic, I haven't got you to this point in the book only to tell you not to start a business. I'm not that cruel.

At the very beginning I told you to start by identifying a customer. This chapter takes that one step further. I am going to suggest that, having shown you can get one customer, you need to start a marketing campaign and demonstrate that you can get customers consistently. Even better, you will be able to work out how much each customer costs to find and then improve your cost per acquisition. This will allow you to see if the campaign is sustainable. A good campaign is the foundation to your business. What could be better than knowing you have a tap for business you can turn on whenever you need it?

Nike

What do you think of when you hear the word Nike?

A surface to air missile system put into operation by the US government in 1953? Perhaps the Greek winged goddess of victory and companion of Zeus who used to fly around battlefields rewarding the victors with glory and fame?

You're almost certainly thinking of Nike Incorporated, the sportswear company that provides a fascinating case study; not because it is a big company but because of how it got started. The founders of Nike started a model business with the utmost efficiency, refusing to spend money where it was not needed, and spotting that their opportunity lay in starting a marketing campaign, not a business.

Let's examine the interesting case of the Nike logo. That famous swoosh does not symbolise a giant tick, but rather it represents the Goddess Nike in flight – it's so obvious when you look at it closely – or maybe not, but I suppose that is what you get when you only pay a student graphic designer $35 and give a limited time frame for completion. For that is exactly what Nike did. By way of contrast, any idea how much was paid for the 2012 Olympic logo? That's right – £400,000.

Long gone are the days when Phil Knight, CEO of Nike, was selling trainers out of the boot of his car and paying student graphic designers to draw giant tick marks (and he really did *both* of these things). Gone also are the days when Coach Bowerman poured rubber into the family waffle iron and invented Nike's very own 'waffle sole'. These times may be gone, but the stories remain immortalised in the mythology that surrounds them, much like the mythical figure the company is named after.

Nike now has a number of senior executives who spend the majority of their time as official 'corporate storytellers'; in fact all new employees have to sit through two days of storytelling to learn the company heritage before they learn how to do their job.

There is method to this madness. It serves two very important functions – not only does it help to integrate the employees and make them feel a sense of belonging, but also encourages them to become Nike's best salespeople. They understand and empathise with the company's mythology. They have a story that works.

Don't Get Started – Get Marketing!

What are the key components to a marketing campaign?

1. Choosing your media. What kind of marketing will you do? An advert, internet pay-per-click, telephone sales? Choose the media you are going to test – ideally you should run tests across several media to see what works the best. Remember you should test, test, and test again.

2. Fixing a start date and an end date – this is crucial. A marketing campaign needs to be clearly defined so that you can assess its success. Run it for a limited time and measure the impact.

3. Coming up with an offer. This needs to be compelling and good value, a 'why would they buy?' proposition. Concentrate on your main proposition, but why not also consider a free or low cost offering to get people hooked?

4. Capturing data. Remember, even if people don't buy, make sure you are capturing their data. Their name, telephone number and email are enough, but the more the

merrier. As your business develops, having a great database is essential, both for sourcing future sales and researching your market.

5. Being sales driven not informative or brand building. A marketing campaign should be designed to result in sales. If you are just brand building or providing information, you're on the wrong track.

6. No long-term contracts or agreements. This is about affordability. Many times I have seen people do an all-or-nothing marketing campaign; putting everything in financially, thinking it is so compelling that it can't fail. Beware! Expect it to achieve a fraction of the forecast: without lots of experimentation, changing of wording, changing of scripts, changing of the target market etc. it will probably massively underperform – so best steer clear.

7. Working out your numbers. When looking at the costings, do the simple maths and ask how many you need to sell to break even and make your marketing campaign worthwhile. Is that feasible? Can you realistically double that?

8. Getting creative with costs. Consider as many low cost and no cost options as possible. Can you mail a partner's customers and give them a cut of sales? Could you pick up the phone and call people yourself? There are many low cost or no cost methods. Remember to split test – this is where you use different copy or scripts and measure the results.

9. Keep putting the bucket down the well. When you find a campaign that does better than break even, keep doing it. Repeat the campaign again and again. This is

what you have been looking for; this is the catalyst to getting started – congratulations!

Market or No Market? That is the Question

What is the first thing you should do well before you even think about getting a logo, registering a domain name or even thinking of a business name?

Correct! You need to make sure that there is even a market out there for whatever it is you are selling – after all, what is the point of selling something that nobody will buy?

Despite this it seems to be a recurring theme that many people new to business get stuck with, so I will lay out a step-by-step guide on how to determine if there is a market or not for what you're selling.

If you are white labelling or re-selling a product for an already successful business then you probably do not need to do this step, as they have already proven that a market exists for their product. But you'll still need to know how to reach the customers, of course.

Why are Competitors a Good Thing?

A common newbie mistake is to get excited when you find that no one else is advertising your idea. However, to think you are the only person in the world to have thought of the idea is somewhat foolish.

Usually the reason why there are no adverts or businesses selling what you want to sell is because someone has tried and failed; they found that there was no market. Put simply, people could not care less about buying it.

If, however, you can find lots of adverts and other people thriving in this market then you know that there is a good chance that this market has some ready-made demand.

Where Should You Look for Adverts?
Start off with magazines catering to the interests of your market; see if there are any ads selling what you wish to sell. If there are, buy the last 12 months' worth of back issues and see which ads have been running the longest.

Cut these out and put them in your swipe file, as these could help you write your own advertising later on.

The cheaper alternative to this is using Google, though you will find that even failed projects on the web can linger about for a few years before the domain names expire, so it can be hard to determine whether it is working for them or not. Magazine ads, on the other hand, are expensive and rarely run consecutively if they are not producing profits.

If you are going to use Google, make sure you pay attention only to the paid ads, the ones that appear on the right-hand side and sometimes at the top.

Get Down and Dirty with Competitor Research
If you are confident that you have found a market that has plenty of vitality and lots of competition, you're well on your way to starting a business. But before you make a product, or even bother giving your business a name, you need to know what you're up against.

You should try and see what the sales process is for your top competitors. Call them and make notes on the sales pitches they use, so that you can familiarise yourself with their selling techniques and marketing strategies.

Sign up for their email lists and direct mail lists; order their product if possible and see if they try and up-sell you anything, how often they send you offers etc.

Do a price comparison to find out what everyone charges for their products and what it is they offer. You can use this to make a more expensive product later on.

Ask the Market What it Wants!

You need to find people that are in the market for your potential product and you need to find out what they want. You can do this by networking, asking questions in online forums or doing a telephone survey of people you know have bought similar products and services.

You will sometimes be surprised at how much of a mismatch there is between what the market really wants and the angle other products are being pitched at. If you find such an angle it can give you a good foothold on the market when you launch your product.

Testing the Market

You need to find a cheap way of testing the market. Usually the best way to do this is to find an affiliate programme or get a white label/re-seller agreement with your competition, and try your hand at selling their product on a commission basis first.

If you can't sell their product and at least break even, you are probably going to have a hard time selling your own and it is probably best to try a different market or improve your selling skills.

Remember, your goal at this stage is not to make money; it is more to prove that there are people willing to spend money on the products or services you are trying to sell and to get a feel for how much volume you could sell.

If you can at least break even during this phase then this should be considered a massive success – it proves there could be a very workable business model in this market. Of course there is a great deal you can still do to refine the process and take sales to the next level.

Starting Your Business

By now you should have found a market, researched your competitors, if possible made at least ten sales of one of your competitors' products, and have a clear idea of what exactly you need to improve on your product or service to make it more appealing than your competitors'.

That done, it's time to get your product made, get a name, a logo etc. But don't waste too much time on this part. Especially don't waste any money, as you are going to need as much as you can get for your marketing budget.

Direct Response versus Branding
If you ask anyone for marketing advice and they start talking about branding, do yourself a favour and turn your ears off – do not listen to a word they say.

We are in the 'direct response' world now; that means we need to make profit when we advertise. Branding is really only in the domain of the larger businesses with scale and market reach. A famous direct response marketer once said (I forget who), the best way to do branding is to just sell a load of your products with a logo on them.

Direct response marketing is simple: you pay 'x' amount for advertising and you get 'y' amount back. If an ad is losing you money, you stop running it; if it's not, you keep running it, simple stuff, hey?

So why would anyone want to spend £30,000 on an ad that gets zero results?

Price and Positioning

You do not need to enter your market as the cheapest option, it is sometimes best to enter the market as the most expensive. The value perceived in your product is purely subjective; you can always add value to allow you to charge a premium price.

If the price of a raw bit of metal is £50, by turning it into a coin you could charge £200. But by packaging that coin in a hermetically sealed box, providing lots of neatly presented information about the history and adding a bit of scarcity, such as 'limited edition, only 200 ever made', you could probably sell them for £1000 each.

How much extra does it cost you for the box, the printed info etc.? Not much. But £200 to £1000 is a lot of extra mark up for this perceived value.

Think what you could do at little cost or with minimal effort to make your product or service more valuable.

Claude Hopkins and Schlitz Beer
Sometimes all it takes to grow to number one in your market is to just tell people what you do. Take the famous case study of Claude Hopkins and Schlitz Beer.

Claude Hopkins, a famous direct response marketer, was called in to help Schlitz Beer gain a bigger market share. All the adverts at the time were pitching the same angle, that the beer was pure beer. Unfortunately, nobody really knew what 'pure' beer was.

After taking a tour at the Schlitz manufacturing plant, Hopkins viewed firsthand the processes of making the beer. These processes were not unique. In fact, every other beer company used the same process – but to an outsider the process was somewhat amazing.

The water came from a 4000-foot-deep well, special filters made out of wood pulp removed the impurities and special rooms with filtered air existed just so that the beer could be cooled down without being contaminated with impurities. The pipes and pumps were cleaned two times a day to prevent any contamination and the glass bottles the beer would end up in were steam cleaned four times before a single drop of beer was poured into them.

The quality standards and the complexity of the process fascinated Hopkins and he asked the managers why they did not tell their prospective customers about all the things they did to make the beer so pure. The reason they gave was that every beer manufacturer used the same processes. They did not think it was that important.

So, in his advertising campaign, Hopkins went on to describe every step in the manufacturing process of this 'nurtured by science beer'. Being the first to tell the story behind how the beer was made took Schlitz Beer from fifth place to position of market leader for a whole generation to come.

This just goes to show that you do not need a unique product, or even a product that no one else can supply cheaper, you just have to be the first to tell the story that others see as too insignificant to tell.

Writing Your First Ad

Before you sit down to write your first ad you have a whole load of research to do. Preparation is the key to success in creating any kind of marketing campaign. By now you should already have a basic idea about your market, and preferably be a customer of the market yourself. If not you will have to take the research steps even more seriously.

Customer Demographics

You need to understand your customer demographics. Not only does this help you target your advertising but it also helps you craft a message that is relevant to your customers, both emotionally and logically.

Demographics include things like age, income, gender, race, home ownership, employment status, location etc.

Customer Jargon and Slang Words

Every industry and market has its own language – industry jargon and slang to help explain things that are only relevant to other people who share those interests. Unless you're selling something for beginners, you need to speak the same language as your market, otherwise they will see you as an outsider.

Understand Your Market

It is critical that you have an inside-out understanding of your market; especially what other people are selling to them and what they have been sold before. Are there a lot of scam products in this market that do not fulfil their promises? If so you will need to craft your message to overcome these objections.

Message to Market Match

Once you have these things in place you should be intimate enough with your market to make sure you tailor a message that is not only relevant to what they want, but also comes across as creditable and pushing the right buttons.

Imagine Who You're Writing to

When writing your ad, imagine you are writing to one person who represents your ideal customer. Write as if you are talking to an old friend; you should always write your ads just as you would speak, using simple language that's clear and not hard to understand. If it is too complicated, no one will stop to try and figure out what you mean, they will just move on.

Bar Stool Example

Imagine you are in a bar and a person a few stools down from you starts talking to the guy behind the bar about a problem that your product solves. What would you say that summarises your product in less than 27 seconds?

Elevator Pitch

This is the most condensed form of your sales message. It should be no more than 27 seconds long. It should be short, concise and to the point. It should make very clear what you do and create an interest in someone that needs your product.

The idea is that you should be able to deliver this pitch in person under even the most time pressured circumstances.

Try using the following template:

We help [[types of people]] to [[achieve results]] even if [[handicap]]

Examples of this template in action might be:

We help baby boomers to build a profitable portfolio in the stock market, even if they have never invested before

or

We help single mums to find jobs that allow them to work at home, even if they have not been in the work force for five years or more

or

We help small business owners outsource their book-keeping even if their accounts are currently a complete mess

What are Your Customers Really Buying?

Counter to popular belief, people do not buy what things *are*, they buy what things *do* – and ultimately they buy things because of how they think owning these things will make them feel.

People do not purchase that £5000 course on becoming wealthy because they want a lot of money; what they really want are the feelings they think having a lot of money will give them, such as attractiveness, power, authority, respect, social status, sexual appeal and a long list of other intangible things.

Women do not buy jewellery because they think it is beautiful, they buy it because they think if they wear it they will look beautiful.

People do not buy a Rolex watch because it keeps better time, they buy it because it makes them feel important, powerful, successful etc.

There is an underlying emotional motive behind every purchase. But you cannot sell on emotion alone: it is a two-layered process. People might very well buy on emotion but emotion is irrational, so you also need to spoon feed them some logical reasons why they should buy your product.

A man might buy a rare coin on the emotional basis that it is limited, has lots of history attached to it and has a fascinating story to tell, but what would he tell his wife? 'It is an investment that will go up in value'.

There are always two reasons why someone buys something – the reason they tell you and the real reason. Always remember that.

Features and Benefits

Theodore Levitt once said, 'Don't sell quarter-inch drills, sell quarter-inch holes'. People do not buy features, they buy benefits. A feature is simply something that your product has, but a benefit is what it does for them. For example, your bookkeeping software has a reporting feature; its benefit is that it allows you to keep control of your finances at a push of a button, reducing costs by as much as 40% and increasing your productivity tenfold. By having this information readily available, you save making financial blunders that could cost you six figures or more.

Make sure it is clear what the benefit of buying the product is to the customer.

Finding Your Hook

Once you have grasped the above concepts it is time to find your hook; this is the thing that grabs your prospects' attention with an outrageous but believable promise or statement, and builds curiosity and readership.

John Carlton, a famous direct response copywriter in the USA, is an excellent example of someone who can come up with good hooks. While doing a promotion for a golf product for one of his clients, and trying to find a hook, he asked the client how he had discovered the particular method that he teaches. The reply was that he had once seen a one-legged golfer hit a ball straighter and further than his two-legged counterparts. From this the hook was born, the headline was: Amazing Secret Discovered By One-Legged Golfer. Adds 50 Yards To Your Drives, Eliminates Hooks And Slices . . . And Can Slash Up To 10 Strokes From Your Game Almost Overnight!

Developing the right hook is the most important part of your marketing campaign and you should spend the most amount of time working on this to come up with something good.

USP – Unique Selling Point
It is not hard to give yourself a USP (unique selling point) even if you are currently selling something that everybody else is. Take, for example, Domino's, which, in the early days, nearly went bankrupt. Adding a USP not only saved the business but catapulted it into the pizza-making giant that it is today.

The USP was, 'Arrives in 30 minutes or less or it is free'. They did not have the best pizza, and they stopped running that offer shortly after due to having to give away too many free pizzas, but it brought them into the awareness of the public consciousness.

Meet Your Prospect Where He or She Already is
When you write your advertising material you must enter the conversation that is already happening in your prospect's

mind. You need to meet the same emotional states that he or she is experiencing and say things that will get them nodding their head in agreement before you slowly lead him or her towards your end goal (which is to get the sale).

If your prospective customer is angry because he or she just caught one of their employees stealing customer data and is looking for security solutions to make sure it cannot happen again, you could lead your ad with something like the following:

> *Is your customer data safe? 74% of all business data theft is carried out by employees who have administrator access to your company files. Using new cloud-based customer relationship management software gives you greater control and security over your vital business data, making sure that only the authorised people within your organisation have access to data they need.*

What Is The Job of The Headline in Your Ad?

To make them read the next line; and the job of the next line is to make them read further into your sales message. Always remember this – it is the key to getting any of your sales messages read. You could have the best product in the world but if no one knows what it will do for them then you will never sell any of it.

Don't Make Your Ad Look Like an Ad

Most ad agencies and small business owners routinely design their adverts to look like other adverts. The instinct is understandable but it's a sure path to losing money. The best performing adverts are always the ones that look like valued content, that blend in with their surroundings rather than blend in with the other advertisements. A full-page ad that looks like an interesting article and delivers useful and interesting content is going to pull more response than a full-page ad that's full of fancy pictures and meaningless slogans. The same principle applies to direct mail; a personal looking letter with a regular stamp and hand writing is more likely to get opened and read than a franked and branded envelope with a PO Box return address printed on the back of it.

Split Testing and Statistical Significance

You should never just write one ad; you need to test and keep testing until you find the one that works the best. The simplest way of doing this is the classic A/B split test. It is important to keep in mind that you should never try and split test more than one element at a time, otherwise this would invalidate the test. So, if you're testing the headline, only change the headline and nothing else in the ad.

You will usually need to expose the ad to a few thousand impressions for it to be statistically significant.

Control Ads

Once you have an advert that is pulling in consistent results on any one given medium, and you are unable to beat it in your split testing, this is now your control ad. Use this ad to find new marketing channels, and if the advert flops and does not work then you know it is the marketing channel that's not suitable rather than your ad that's not working. This is a powerful tool for scalability.

The Lessons to be Gained from this Chapter

- Don't start a business, start a marketing campaign.
- Reserve the right to change your marketing activity if it's not working. So no long-term contracts!
- Determine the size of your market. Does your customer exist, and will he or she be interested?
- Get down and dirty with competitor research. What works for your rivals?
- Find your hook. What promise or statement can you make to secure your customers' attention?
- Concentrate on making sales, not branding.
- Get the advertising right. Try different approaches and see what works best. You'll get there eventually, and the customers will follow.

CHAPTER 10

A COMPELLING
OFFER

The Ingredients of a Compelling Offer

A compelling offer is marketing come good; it's when the sales techniques and promotional material you've designed come together to make a package that interests customers. In order to make a compelling offer you need to make sure you have all the correct ingredients. Here is a list of the must-haves in any sales pitch, whether it be a sales letter, video or personal presentation.

1. Hook/headline/elevator pitch
2. Lead in
3. Features and benefits
4. Testimonials
5. Scarcity
6. Risk reversal
7. Call to action
8. PS/summary

1. Hook/headline/elevator pitch – This is where you have to grab your prospects' attention and build interest and curiosity.

2. Lead in – There is nothing like a good story to build some credibility, but make it relevant. If your story is boring or off topic this will not help you. The story should demonstrate the value of the product and be centred around a real life tale (whether the central character is you or one of your customers). It should describe how the problem your product will solve was encountered and demonstrate how the solution was found.

3. Features and benefits – We have already covered what the difference is between a feature and a benefit. You need to make sure you have written down and fleshed out all the possible benefits your product has to offer before you go about pitching your product.

4. Testimonials – You must make sure you have a stock of testimonials ready to hand. If it's a new product, consider doing some deals at cost just so you can get the feedback. A positive success story or case study can go a long way in showing prospective customers that the product works for people just like them.

5. Scarcity – Every compelling offer has a degree of scarcity whether it is limited supply, a discount that ends by a certain date, or even a free bonus report that is only available for a limited amount of time. The scarcity has to be real and you have to honour the cut off date, otherwise you will lose the attention of the market. So, make sure your scarcity is genuine and that the important details are transmitted clearly to the customer.

6. Risk reversal – The biggest objection is risk. If you can reverse the risk for your clients then you have a higher

chance of closing the deal right there and then. You can offer a no questions asked full refund guarantee if they don't like the product, and the longer the guarantee, the fewer returns as they feel under no rush to return the item. This can be hard to implement with service-based businesses but works really well for product-focused operations.

7. Call to action – After delivering your perfect pitch you need to tell the customer what to do next. Whether in person or in print, this is the stage where most people chicken out and never ask for the order. If you do not ask the customer to take action there and then, the chances are they won't, and you have lost them forever. Follow up your hard work and seal the deal.

8. PS/summary – At the end of a sales message you should always summarise your offer: the main benefits and the call to action. Research demonstrates that the summary is generally the second most read part of any letter, aside from the headline, and when talking to someone face to face it's that final summing up that will stick in their memory. So, make sure you get it right.

Offer Instalments on High Ticket Items

It has been shown that if someone is willing to spend £97 on an item, they would also be willing to buy an item for £291 if the payments were spread monthly at £97 without too much effect, and in some cases no effect whatsoever, on conversion rates. Therefore, it follows that if you offer payment in instalments you will get more sales, as well as a small amount of residual income.

High Ticket versus Low Ticket

In some cases an increase in sales has been achieved just by increasing the price! It may sound counterintuitive but a lot of people see more expensive items as being better quality. You should always test having a high ticket item as you may be devaluing your position by offering things too cheaply.

Social Proof

People like doing or buying things that they see other people doing or buying; that is a simple fact of life. If your customer can see social proof of your product's popularity, that people just like them are using and benefiting from it, they will want to have it too.

Make Sure You Have a Solid Sales System

If you only have one front end product to sell you don't really have a business, well not one that would survive any real competition anyway. The easiest person to sell to is someone that has bought a product or service from you before and is happy with the experience. So, make sure that you have other relevant stuff to sell them.

Many businesses lose money or break even on the first sale just so they can get the customer on file and make money on the back end promotions they send to them. While I can't recommend losing money on the first sale, any advertising or acquisition source that breaks even on the front end product should be kept running to build your customer list.

Break Even on the First Sale

Aim to at least break even on the first sale. If you plan to be making the majority of your money on the back end, this allows you to expand your advertising to the wider media. Your competitors, who are selling only one product, simply cannot afford such extensive advertising, which gives you faster growth opportunities.

Back end

This is the term used for a product you offer your customers once they have already bought from you. It should, of course, be highly related and synergistic with the first sale: if you were selling blue cogs, for example, you could follow up with a guide on how to make blue cogs last up to 40% longer.

OTO – One-Time Offers

Immediately after a customer has purchased something is the time they are most likely to buy something else. In this case, a one-time offer that is only available if they act now is very effective, especially if there is some genuine scarcity, such as 50% off or the product never being offered again.

Up-sell

This is when you offer a high ticket item to customers who have purchased a lower ticket item. This works very well with one-time offers and can increase your short-term average customer value quite dramatically.

Down-sell
This is usually a fairly easy sell where you offer the customer another product that is lower in price to the previous offer. It can be used as a one-time offer directly after purchase and when they decline the up-sell.

Pipeline

Running an effective and planned pipeline for customer and prospect follow up is critical if you want constant and measurable income from your database. This is basically a series of planned offers that go out on predetermined dates, which you can test for maximum profit potential.

Prospect Pipeline
When someone shows interest or makes an enquiry but does not buy from you, they are now what is known as your prospect. You should keep a prospect file and remove entries when they become customers or request that you no longer contact them again.

You should send out offers to your prospect file every now and then to tempt them into becoming customers. Try and increasingly make the offers more tempting and do anything you can to encourage them to spend their first pound with you: once you get them to part with any amount of money it is going to be much easier to get more business out of them.

Customer Pipeline
Make sure you follow up with your customers regularly. Maybe send an offer for a new product you have every three

weeks or so: repeat buyers are where the money is. Try and segment your lists so that you can find the people who only purchased one item from you and use the same tactic you use with prospects – increasingly attractive and high-value offers – to try and lure them into making a second purchase.

Customer Lifetime Value

Once you have been running your marketing campaign for a while you should have an idea about how much money on average you make from a customer in the first 60-days and over their purchasing lifetime. It may be the case that each customer, on average, spends £1000 with you over a 60-day period. Even if your front end product is only £97 you can spend a lot more than that to get a customer, you can even spend £500 per customer because you know you will make double that back over a 60-day period. This allows you to compete in very competitive markets and crush your competition, who are still trying to make money on the first sale. That's why, as I said before, if you try and make all your money on the first sale you do not really have a business and it is very hard for you to compete when someone comes in and does it properly.

Customer Lists and CRM Systems

Whatever you use to manage your customer lists – paper, spreadsheets or CRM system – you need to treat your customer lists like gold, and you need to record as much information as you can, as this will assist you in your marketing efforts.

Newsletter

If you are serious about your business you should run a free newsletter, whether it is weekly, monthly or quarterly. You should never pitch from your newsletter but deliver valuable and useful content that will help your customers and is related to the product or service you are selling. This is a chance to build your reputation, show your personality and build rapport with your customers to ensure long-term business.

Landing Pages

If you're going to drive traffic to a website, make sure you have a specially designed page. Do not send customers and prospects to your home page and expect them to know what to do, because they will just leave. Preferably you should have a page with a headline, some bullet points and a form they can fill out to get a free downloadable report, this is to gather prospect data that you can follow up with to turn prospects into customers. It is important to make sure that whatever you give them provides them with enough value and builds creditability or they will not do business with you.

Video Sales Pages

If you are going to deliver a pitch for your product by video make sure that you use the sequence in the format described under the heading 'The Ingredients of a Compelling Offer'.

This is a good sequence to use to help build your case and try to close the deal. An easy and cost-effective way to make sales presentations – without having to pay any crazy fees to a professional video guy who would most likely want £5000 upfront and know little about how to make a video convert – is to make a PowerPoint presentation and use some screen casting software to record the screen as you play it, while talking over the presentation.

Lead Generation versus Direct Selling

Depending on your selling model you may choose to sell directly with a payment button on your website or an order form on your direct mail letters – or you can go down the route of collecting leads instead and follow up with them in person or by phone.

Although following up by phone is less automated, if you're a good salesperson you will get a lot more bang for your buck and get a lot more money back from your advertising efforts. Also, if you are not yet skilled at selling in print, it can be a lot easier to go for the leads than present a full-blown sales pitch in print or video: you only have to make them curious and offer something of high perceived value for giving you their details.

Social Media

It seems that everybody is still excited about the whole social media movement, but you have to remember that the selling strategy is very different from that of direct mail, face to face and phone. You should never try and pitch anything directly in social media; instead you should direct them to some free content where they can opt in for more information, entering your sales funnel that way. There are literally hundreds of social media sites, possibly even thousands. Some of the more popular ones you should look into include Twitter, Facebook, LinkedIn and Google Plus.

Viral Marketing

Getting free viral traffic to your business from the web is achieved by giving high value content away for free. There are several different media you can use:

Blog

If you update a blog frequently with content you can get a lot of search engine, social media and return traffic; it is perhaps the most time-intensive method but some people do enjoy it. If you feel this is for you then give it a try; you can get a free copy of Wordpress to install on your website and use as a blogging platform or create a blog on ecademy.

Video

If you have good video footage, that can also go viral. Place it up on one of the many video channels, YouTube being one of the most popular, or use a service like Traffic Geyser to syndicate all your videos.

Viral PDF Reports

This is my favourite method: compile a really good white paper, convert it into PDF format and give it out; it will sit on people's computers, driving return traffic as well as getting sent to friends.

Refer a Friend Scripts

There are many refer a friend scripts out on the market. Best placed under any valuable content that you are giving away for free, this allows people to drive referral traffic right to the page they are on.

Affiliate Marketing

This basically allows you to recruit people to sell your products and services on a commission only basis; there are many affiliate marketing services out there you can use. A good affiliate management program will allow you to track and manage affiliates and track payments. This can be a good way to get extra sales but you have to be generous with the commission and provide a high converting sales page for them to drive traffic to in order for it to work.

Credibility

Establishing credibility when first starting out can be the biggest obstacle. This can most easily be overcome by writing a book about the area that you're doing business in; this will help establish you as an expert and can be given to prospects to build your credibility.

Joint Ventures

This is an excellent way to grow your business if you can find someone you are not in direct competition with but who has an existing large customer base of people who are likely to want your product. You can use such joint ventures to grow your customer and prospect base.

You can either ask them to email their database to you or to send a direct mail letter to their customers with a cover note recommending your product or service. If they send out monthly bills by post, for example, you can even have your sales materials, such as a flyer, included to save on postage costs.

Email Marketing

It would be wise to collect email addresses from prospects and customers as it is a cheap way to stay in touch. Make sure you do not mail them too often though or the response rate will get very low. If collecting email addresses from your website, I would recommend using an auto responder service such as GetResponse or Aweber to handle your list.

Tele Marketing

Cold calling may not be the nicest way to get prospects and customers but if you are starting out it can be the cheapest way. To rent a targeted list you can expect to pay anywhere between 0.10p and 0.30p per record: usually a minimum order is 1000 records. If using a 27-second elevator pitch to collect an email address to send them a free report, you can expect a 1:10 record conversion; so 1000 records should give you about 100 prospects. How many of those you convert into customers will depend on your sales skill and the efficiency of your sales process.

The Lessons to be Gained from this Chapter

- Get every component of your sales pitch right.
- Reduce the risk for your customer and you've a better chance of making the sale.
- Seal the deal! Make sure you end on a high note and get the crucial handshake.
- Be flexible with your offer but make sure you always break even.
- Think about your customers' lifetime value, not just that first sale.
- Explore ways of communicating with your customers, with newsletters, social media and viral marketing.

CHAPTER 11

There's a popular business saying, 'How do you eat an elephant?' – to which the answer is, 'One mouthful at a time'. It's a phrase generally associated with time management, but it's very useful for us when facing any big obstacle; and starting a business is certainly that.

In this final chapter we are going to take what we have learnt in this book and use it to show how to work your way through the vast-seeming task of setting up a business using self-determined goals and timetables, so that you can take all the encouragement contained between these covers and make a start on what might be the most exciting challenge of your life.

After all, this book is about self-development not shelf-development (don't just leave it on your shelf with the others); it is a call to action, not just a source of information.

Chances are you bought this book because you have been actively thinking about starting that long-thought-about business, so now is your best opportunity to take the contents here as a friendly shove and start doing it.

You really are the only thing that is holding you back; the sooner you take action the better, don't look back!

Timetable

Mapping out the next three months of your life is not so easy, but I've divided up your time into a series of simple, time-based objectives so that you can begin to put into practice the planning you've started and get your business up and running. Your mission, should you choose to accept it, is to take your calendar and pencil in the following deadlines – my three-month timetable to getting you started. It's structured around achievable goals in achievable time frames, so that you can plan to work your way through a series of empowering, practical tasks, all of which will take you nearer to your destination. None will exhaust you, and each is a little win, and a small step forward.

Just because some look easy, don't cram too many in or feel tempted to rush forward; I want you to feel like you are finding this a bit too simple, and as if you could have got started already. That is the point – what you previously interpreted as a huge mountain to climb should begin to resemble a simple series of speed bumps on life's highway. I have spent much of this book trying to explain that it's easier than people think to make the leap – hopefully the use of this timetable will really bring that home.

In the timetable I have outlined you'll cover some of the key milestones we have talked about so far, but remember that for your particular business there may be other key milestones, like obtaining permissions, signing agency agreements and leases, or getting licences or accreditations. If you need to build other targets into the deadline, don't panic – simply go back to that exercise I outlined earlier in the book where you list the reasons why you are not ready now, and try to split these into small chunks to put into your timetable. The three-month schedule I've outlined can be adjusted if you have complex tasks to add in, but, if you can, keep three months in mind, because it's perfectly possible to do all you need to do in that time frame.

Then, once the commitment has been made, you need to make sure you move heaven and earth to hit these time frames. This is your first step into entrepreneurship, so treat it seriously – start making excuses and missing deadlines now and you're setting yourself a bad example for the future. If you really struggle, try outsourcing your motivation – get a coach or a loved one to keep a copy of your timetable and nag you on a routine basis, or break down tasks further by putting daily tasks in your diary to ensure that you are focused on meeting the milestones that are approaching. In short, you know how you work, so try and make this fit with your way of getting stuff done, and then just Go Do.

We're going to set six target dates, starting from right now. By each milestone you will have taken your business a series of crucial steps forward. The first milestone is only a week away, so allow yourself a moment to take that fact in. After that, we'll be working towards further milestones: two weeks, one month, six weeks, two months and, finally, three months. You'll be in business sooner than you ever thought imaginable.

Before you begin, have you made time in your life to get this done? I mentioned before that you'll sometimes need to make a diary appointment with yourself and make sure you stick to it. You know your own circumstances and commitments, and you know what you'll need to sacrifice in order to free up the time to get started. If you just add these tasks to an already busy life, then as soon as it becomes challenging or you have a boring bit to do (hopefully none of it will be too boring when you consider what the outcome is) you will be tempted to focus your energies elsewhere. So make sure you have as much time as you can possibly spare to devote to this.

Remember, if you don't give it 100% it won't work, so find a way to give this the attention it deserves.

Above all, calm down, take a deep breath and relax. You just need to take that first step.

MILESTONE ONE: Week One

You're seven days into your journey. By this time you should have done nothing more than worked back through the pen and paper activities we completed in Chapter 9.

This means mapping out some time, thinking about your market and your product, and thinking about how you're going to reach your customers. What will your price point be, what kind of margin will you expect to make and how would you describe your product or service solution in an elevator pitch? As you progress through the next milestones, you'll be testing every single one of these thoroughly, so the goal here is not to spend time on detailed research, but instead to record what you already know and intend to do going forward. As you progress you'll find that your instincts were good in some areas, miles off in others, and in need of corroborating evidence more often than not. That's fine – in the first week you're just feeling your way towards a business plan, and you should try to enjoy this process. It should give you an overview of what comes next and, hopefully, inspire you along the way. Go with the answers that feel right to you.

Why are we starting with this, when having not yet put our business into action we're not necessarily in possession of all the facts we need to populate it? Because the act of writing things down is hugely liberating. I often start a day with an overwhelming mass of things flying around in my head; they are all important and they all have deadlines. By writing them down you get to see all of the things clearly set out and can start to formulate your plan of attack. It is like your brain goes into a sort of survival mode, worrying that you will forget something. The act of writing it down gives your brain a break from trying to juggle all the things you have to remember and frees it up to start solving the issues one at a time. By completing this task in the first week you'll be much better equipped for the next set of milestones – and you will have a much greater sense of your business.

MILESTONE TWO: Week Two
By the end of week two you will have road tested your product or service definition, and you will have spoken in detail to at least five people in your target demographic (not family or friends).

Your product definition is vitally important; it demonstrates that you have thought through exactly what it is you're offering and enables others to immediately understand it.

Of course, it is a reality that many businesses actually change or adapt their product as they go. When I started my telecoms company I had a clear product definition: the provision of personal numbers that stayed with the customer rather than being lost when he or she moved or switched mobile phones. But technology is a fast-moving area and, while the market matured, I found that the success of my sideline operation, providing mobile phones and landline phone services, grew beyond my expectations and, pretty quickly, the revenue and profit from the 'sideline' services far exceeded that from the 'core' personal numbering product.

As with many things in life, plans change and products and services adapt. My original product definition needed revising, but that's as it should be – in fact if you do find yourself needing to revise your product offering, it's a sign that you're paying close attention to what the market wants and responding to it. Far better that than to stick stubbornly to a product that never hits the mark in the first place, or has become out of date.

But don't worry about that now – your goal here is to describe what you are doing right now, or will be doing when you get going. What is your product, and how will it work?

This definition is inextricably tied to your market research. So make sure that you put aside time this week (marking it out in advance in your diary) to take the opportunity to talk to people in your target demographic and sound them out. You need to listen to their desires, explain your product and obtain their enthusiastic buy-in, because if you are unable to sell them the idea of the product then you need to rethink, at the very least, how you present it and – more importantly – perhaps even the product itself.

Work out what your point of difference is, what your USPs are and what the key differentiator is that sets your product apart. The key is to understand whether or not that point of difference actually means anything to your customer. Apply the term 'so what?' to your idea – does it really benefit your end user?

As previously mentioned, the target customer of my telecoms business was a small to medium sized company which used between five and 50 mobile phones. This was an interesting space as these customers had much higher than average monthly bills, as compared to individuals who just used phones socially and corporate customers who would carefully manage their employees' usage. In a smaller business, mobile phones were an essential tool, and brought about massive efficiencies.

Our differentiator was that instead of having to go to a mobile phone shop and queue up with the screaming babies in pushchairs and all the normal customers, or else call the network directly and deal with someone in a call centre, we gave them their own account manager who would add phones, cancel phones, deliver phones, monitor usage and suggest tariff changes; generally act as a sort of outsourced telecoms manager for their business. No one else was doing that at the time and it gave us great and loyal customers.

We did not know this immediately. In fact, we only found this out by trial and error and spent many wasted months trying to sell a worse business proposition. I hadn't done my research, but you have the benefit of my experience here and can avoid making that mistake. Ask potential clients – taking care not to weight the question in your favour – if the differentiator you have identified is as valuable to them as you think it will be. Gauge the feedback carefully.

The things I felt were most important when starting out in my business many years ago – like the provision of personal numbers – turned out to be less important than I thought. Until we understood what really motivated our customers, we were unable to truly compete. Once we knew, we dominated. The sooner you realise what key differentiator you can harness to dominate in your market, the better you'll do.

When talking to potential customers, make sure that you don't fall into the trap of investing value in the opinion of the wrong people. During this week you need to speak to at least five people – that's a conservative number and you'll preferably reach out to more – but crucially make sure that these people are representative, relevant and not biased one way or the other. Do whatever you need to do to get to speak to them, and pitch as if you want their business.

Listen very carefully to what they say – it is very easy to get caught up in your own idea and forget to take feedback, or else to take exception to their opinion. But criticism at this stage is a positive thing. How can you adapt your proposition so it is not judged so harshly? Make sure that you ask them what their ideal supplier would offer, and see if you are missing something key in your proposition.

I did not listen anywhere near enough in the beginning, and had I got my pitch right very early on I would have been much more successful.

In my most recent business, the Harbour Club – where I teach people how to buy and sell distressed companies – I sat down with potential customers and gave them the pitch. This time I got two immediate customers, and for a product that costs tens of thousands of pounds. I knew I had hit the nail on the head with regards to a compelling proposition and something that delivered real value to the customer, and it was easy to roll out from there.

You may not get your two customers that easily – but I guarantee that the feedback you do get will be invaluable. It will enable you to further hone your product description and know your market. It's a vital stage in the process. If you're thorough and attentive, you can spend this week having as many conversations as possible, testing your product and definition and refining them with each bout of feedback. You'll know a great deal more about your business by the time you've finished.

Go back and look at the planning document you put together in week one. How different is your product description now? Are you getting a feel for your pitch? It's important that you keep revisiting it; with each conversation you have you should be getting better at describing just what makes your business proposition so bloomin' marvellous. Keep that document updated and keep it evolving. It'll change a lot more before you hit your three-month target.

MILESTONE THREE: The First Month
By the end of the first four-week period of getting your business up and running, you need to have taken the next step; getting

*your product offering more fleshed out by calculating pricing
policy/price list and working out your margin.*

Price testing is really interesting. We all have our own perception of what an acceptable price is, and too often this clouds our testing. Look hard at your competitors' pricing, look at different price points and work out what the market will bear.

See if you can push those prices up, as I did all those years ago, raising the price of my amusement machines from £1999 for three to £2999. Just like selling a second-hand car, it is easy to reduce a price but almost impossible to put it up! So now is the time to explore pricing and reach an informed conclusion on what the market can stand.

Don't fall into the trap of pricing as you go; have a price list that works and that you stick to. It is a great reference tool for a customer and defends you from relentless negotiation. If you go to a market in North Africa, no price tag means the seller is up for an argument – and all power to them. A price tag, on the other hand, means 'hand over the correct money'. As a business owner, I know which model I prefer.

The final part is your margin. It's hard to quantify exactly what a good margin is, but you need enough of a margin and enough volume to make the business work for you as well as the customer. It sounds blindingly obvious but the key is you need more money in than out, and to have enough leeway to prepare yourself for unseen obstacles.

Once you have your pricing, just do a sanity check.

How much does it cost you to get a customer, how much do the goods cost and how much do you sell the goods for? How many do you have to sell to cover your overheads?

Now consider what happens if it costs you four times as much as you think to get a customer. How certain are you of the cost of reaching your market? Remember when I said how logic gets really twisted in business? Well this is one of the areas where you will make or break your business – the cost of getting a customer always seems to defy logic! Once you have customers coming in, you can tweak and tweak it to get the cost down, but initially you need to be very careful.

Don't underestimate the time input. How much of your hard-won time will you have to invest in getting each customer over the line? Remember, you want to grow this business, so if you have to pay people to do this extra communication it can get very expensive, and could make your business hard to grow. Therefore, test and test this area and get a number you can be certain of.

Many businesses I go into now, looking at turnaround, don't actually know what it costs them to get a sale. I have often heard people say, 'Well, we give the salesman 10%'. That may be true, but you also pay the salesman's salary, travel, phone, computer desk and leads for him, through advertising or Google pay-per-click etc. So, when you fully load this cost, you often find businesses are paying to take customers on, not profiting from them. Usually you'll find that a small increase in sales would cover it, but that is not what they have, so they keep pushing on, hoping to sell more while going deeper and deeper into the red.

Please don't allow yourself to get into that position! Start with this knowledge and avoid the mistakes of the masses.

MILESTONE FOUR: Six Weeks

By this point you should have produced a cash flow forecast for the first 90 days of trading, showing income and expenses, and that the business works within those parameters.

How will you manage your cash flow? Cash is king, and now that you have put together your product plan and market research it's time to think about how you'll be operating on a day-to-day basis. Decisions taken early on about the process are important because they set a tone for the future. Decide early if you are going to offer credit terms to customers, for example. This is not so common and probably best ignored when dealing with private individuals, but in the business to business arena it's commonly done, and is a very tempting way to get sales in. Many do it, but take care as this is one of the biggest ways I have ever seen of creating cash starvation. After all, a sale is not a sale until it is paid for.

When providing credit terms ask yourself, 'Would I lend this person/company that amount of money?' If the answer is no, don't provide credit. Look at credit-checking software for new customers, write a policy for offering terms and stick to it. So, for example, you might say that you insist on taking the first three orders cash up front (often referred to as pro forma), the next three orders with a 50% upfront balance and the rest payable seven days after delivery, then seven day terms or fourteen day terms, or whatever you fancy. After a year, once the customer is established, you can go to 30 day terms.

It is a fact of life that if you offer credit you will experience bad debt. If a customer does not pay a £10,000 bill and your margin is 50%, the next £20,000 of sales is wasted, you just stand still, so you need to be absolutely on top of the cash and be really strict. If you provide terms, chase it in relentlessly, you need to get it into your bank account as quickly as possible.

For that reason, it's essential that you get your cash flow document going. Accountants and business advisors always recommend a three-year cash flow, but to be honest you won't know until you're up and running exactly what it will look like in three weeks' time, let alone three years, so I recommend simply doing a 90-day forecast, to cover the first 90 days of trading.

A cash flow document need not be terrifying. Open a spread-sheet: put an income section at the top, an expenditure section underneath and – importantly – your bank balance at the bottom. All the key information, big and small, about how you are paying for your business, from rental equipment to electricity bills, through phone lines and your marketing budget, goes into this document, as does every penny that comes back in. It goes without saying that the money coming in should exceed the money going out. A very simple example of a cash flow document is given, which includes a set of typical terms for a start up. It's available for download if you go to www.jeremyharbour.com, click on Go Do and go to the resources page, where you'll find a copy. Unless you want to start from scratch, I suggest you use it as a template for your own document.

	15-Sep	22-Sep	29-Sep	6-Oct	13-Oct	20-Oct	27-Oct	3-Nov
	£	£	£	£	£	£	£	£
Firm orders								
ABC Ltd	12,000			**2,000**		1,000		5,000
123 Ltd			5,000		2,000		1,000	
Acme Ltd		3,250	28,000		1,000			
Jeremy				1,000				
Harbour Ltd	500	500	500	500	500	500	500	500
Total	12,500	3,750	33,500	3,500	3,500	1,500	1,500	5,500
Operating payments								
Key suppliers								
Supplier A		2,500				2,500		2,500
Manufacturer					5,000			
Raw Material		5,000					5,000	7,000
payroll	500	500	500	500	500	500	500	500
freight		200		200		200		200
Electricity		7,162						
Rent			2,000				2,000	
Rates			1,000				1,000	
Phone		286		83	292			
Sales Tax							12,000	
Payroll tax	300	300	300	300	300	300	300	300
Total	800	13,448	6,300	1,083	6,092	3,500	20,800	10,500
Other items – overdraft								
Total other	0	0	0	0	0	0	0	0
Net movement for week	11,700	(9,698)	27,200	2,417	(2,592)	(2,000)	(19,300)	(5,000)
Opening bank balance	0	11,700	2,002	29,202	31,619	29,027	27,027	7,727
Closing bank balance	**11,700**	**2,002**	**29,202**	**31,619**	**29,027**	**27,027**	**7,727**	**2,727**

The expenses entered in the document are, of course, hypo-thetical. Every business is different – you may have costs for website development, marketing and a whole host of other things, so write up your own wish list, then fill in the boxes. At the bottom you will have a running bank balance.

Now you can quite simply move things around until you get to a position where the balance at the bottom works. If you get more sales in early on, you can accelerate some of the spending.

The key question is, with the cash flow completed, can you afford it? Does the balance at the bottom work with your finances? If not, can payments be moved around so it does work? If they can't, can you get the finance elsewhere? You might be better off simply reassessing your budget demands and remembering that it's perfectly possible to be creative about how you can start with as little capital as possible. That frugal nature will serve you well as the business grows. Of course, as that happens, juggling the financials will become more complex, as more and more variables become involved. But you will learn as you go, and as the financial demands become greater so will your comfort and ease in navigating your spreadsheet.

When I started my first business, the bank asked me for an income and expenditure list, a sort of monthly costs versus income report. It was very basic, a system that works on a fundamental level but lacks sophistication and the kind of flexibility that allows you to try out new scenarios.

When I had the telecoms company, the bank asked me for a three-year cash flow. This meant going into a lot more detail, and I did – but only because I had to, and very aware that, because I was dealing so far in advance, most of it was total guesswork. In short, I didn't appreciate its value.

Now, years later, I understand that, used properly and on a rolling short-term basis, your cash flow forecast is your best friend. Everything goes in and nothing goes out that is not in the forecast; no impulse buys, no early payments – use it as your guide and it will revolutionise your cash management. When times are tough, you can juggle the payments out so that it all fits, and communicate clearly with your suppliers so they know exactly when they will get paid. Do this and you'll be able to avoid those 'the cheque is in the post' conversations. This really will reduce stress and give you lots of free time to get on with growing your business.

You will also get early warning of any possible problems, like a big tax bill looming or other things you need to be ready for. When I started, it was a case of the squeaky wheel got the oil, so whoever made the most noise got paid! This then has a terrible effect later on, when you can't cover other payments.

Thankfully I know better now. And now, so do you.

Working out the cash flow is the biggest challenge of this two-week period, but don't panic. So long as you list every expense and make a reasonably accurate prediction, you'll be absolutely fine. What this is really about is nothing more, or less, than learning how to live within your means. And if you haven't learned the basic principles of that by now then it's a good time to start.

Once you've done this, move on to getting a few more essentials in place. Fixing on your business name and making it official is not just an important step, it's a reason to celebrate. Get your trading name decided, register your company and your website URL, and open up your bank account. This is effectively the birth of your business and the christening all rolled into one! So do take a moment to wet the baby's head and have a small glass of bubbly (or orange juice!), but remember not to over-do it as there is much left to do.

Choosing a name for your business can be tricky, but perhaps I'm underestimating you. In fact, I bet you already have it, don't you? If not, then use this milestone to make a decision – remember that lots of people put a lot of thought and time into a name, but there are plenty of great companies with boring names – a cool name does not necessarily equate to a cool business.

Picking your name is something only you can do, but go for something memorable and searchable, making sure that clear and easy to remember domain names are available. Remember to register all the URL variants that you want or can afford within your budget.

With many businesses nowadays the URL you choose can turn out to be one of your most valuable assets, once you have reputation and traffic going to it. So pick something easy to remember, easy to spell and not too long. Don't forget to set up your email so you can send and receive emails from yourname@yournewurl.com.

Now set up your company and make it official. That may sound hard, but in fact the process can be done entirely online, which is a huge bonus for speed and efficiency. In the UK I have used companywizard.com for this purpose, but there are many providers if you want to search. The process is straightforward and inexpensive, and will provide you with your Certificate of Incorporation and Memorandum and Articles of Association, both of which you will need when you head to your bank to open an account.

Most UK banks want to meet you to open a business account, so call ahead and arrange a meeting. They are all as bad as each other, so it does not matter who you go with! Initially you will need a shareholder and a director – I recommend you go on as both. You can add more later but certain things like opening a bank account and getting merchant services are easier with just one director and shareholder. If you have bad credit, then maybe look for a partner to get started with and add yourself later. Bizarrely, although in law a limited company is a seperate legal entity, banks seem to ignore the law and credit check the directors. So if one director has some 'experience' this can count against the whole company – take care to know everything you must in advance, know the rules and work with them.

When you go to meet the bank, take a one-page business explanation, as well as the Certificate of Incorporation, the Memorandum and Articles of Association and a mock up of a letter head. Also take your cash flow forecast, some ID, a utility bill and, of course, your passport – even if you already bank with them.

If you need to accept credit card payments, also ask the bank for a merchant services number. It's advisable to play down how much you will take on cards or, more diplomatically, be as pessimistic as possible, as banks view this as risk, so focus on the small start. If you do loads of transactions later on you can always apologise. Sometimes it's better to ask for forgiveness than permission.

Take a deep breath. You're a business owner.

MILESTONE FIVE: Two Months

You're motoring now. By this stage you should have created your first marketing campaign and revisited your cash flow document in light of marketing expenses. Check you're going to break even. List all sales channels and have a plan of action for each. And have your business cards printed and your sales pitch rehearsed to within an inch of your life.

The cash flow document you put together will have contained a marketing budget – a plan for how to reach your customers and build your business. Now is the time to start using that budget to create and place adverts, network with potential customers and fellow businesses, and begin to get your product known.

If you closely follow the guidelines in Chapter 10, you should have a great little plan ready to go. Your goal is to have a tested set of channels and messages to bring you business at a known cost, so that you can simply 'turn on the tap' and get business.

It took me many, many years to get businesses to do this – often marketing was something I did in sporadic bursts when we needed more sales. In my more recent businesses, a lot of thought and planning goes into creating the customer journey – a pipeline or process that the customer follows. Each stage gives them more information and an opportunity to buy, reducing physical time spent per sale and creating something that can be easily grown. Without this in place it can be very tiring, always fire fighting and reacting to your marketing. In the long term you'll want a marketing plan that provides you with a regular stream of customers.

Right now, your ambitions are on a smaller scale. When you phoned around the competition, asking for prices, where did you see them advertising? Be sensible at this early stage, and don't over-commit. But nor should you be scared to think out of the box. If your competitors are missing a trick marketing wise, there is all the more opportunity for you.

In terms of your sales channels, you can refer back to the brainstorming activity we covered in Chapter 9 and reviewed in the first milestone stage. What you want is a clear breakdown of how you can sell your product and which avenues hold the most potential. If you know that you won't be selling door-to-door, you can cross that off. Will you get your stock shelved in department stores? Can you sell over the telephone? Think about this and clarify what your channels are.

Few of us, when starting a business, have many people besides ourselves to sell the product. Do you have help? Don't worry if you don't – it will come. When I started the telecoms company I had me and me alone! Then I had a shop and me, and after a few years we had developed a whole range of sales channels, from a tie up with Costco to be in all their stores, to a call centre partner selling our products for us, right through to re-sellers who sold our products and re-sellers who white labelled our products and sold them as their own. There are so many different channels that it is worth really thinking about what works best for you.

Some businesses have solely indirect channels like agents and re-sellers; some have solely direct channels like retail and internet. Make sure that if you are in both they don't compete. Franchises or setting up sales territories are a great way to expand your reach, but exercise control so that you don't have too many people competing with your product or risk cannibalising your own sales.

Obviously when you use a direct channel you pay for all the marketing, but you keep all the margin. When you go indirect you save on marketing but lose margin. A good indirect channel can add sales you would not have otherwise got and help you expand quickly, but you need to be sure you are not dependent on a single source of business, or this can make it very risky going forwards.

It goes without saying that putting all your eggs in one basket can be risky, but so can spreading yourself too thinly. Think carefully about which sales model works best, and how your competitors thrive – or miss a trick. By doing this exercise you'll be able to focus on your selling priorities and know how best to use your marketing budget.

And take care, at this stage, to revisit your cash flow document. Is your marketing budget realistic? If not, now is the time to make some changes.

Lastly, spend a bit of time getting ready for your moment to shine. Get some business cards made up and start rehearsing that pitch to within an inch of your life. Work out how to get talking about your business with other people; whether they are potential customers or fellow businesspeople who can provide a valuable sounding board.

You will surely have heard the old adage, 'it is not what you know, it is who you know'. This is often used with derogatory 'old boys' network' connotations, but I am afraid to say that in the world of business, nothing truer has ever been said.

Your success or failure in your business will most likely come down to who you know and who you get to know. Every pound, dollar, euro or yen you will ever make is in someone else's pocket right now.

Talking to people is essential. You need to say what you do and make people aware of your activities. You will be amazed at what happens when you start talking about what you are doing. All these signposts just pop up and show you the way. It is quite amazing that we judge each other so much by what we do, because ultimately you can say you do whatever you like. You can be an actor, just waiting for that first part, and no one will ask to see a formal qualification as proof. And the good news is that when you tell people you run a modest start-up, you're telling the absolute truth. So whatever you do, don't keep it a secret – tell the world.

You need to eat, sleep and breathe your new business now, so your Facebook profile, your LinkedIn profile, everything outward-facing about you now needs to say what you do. You now need to network, to get the message spread far and wide.

Of course, you also need an outcome from your networking, so you might agree that you are looking for a direct customer or a route to market from the list above, or even a supplier. Now pick up your mobile phone (mine has a couple of thousand contacts in) and start at A. Speak to people you have not spoken to for ages. Ask them what they are doing, can you help them in any way? Explain what you are doing and say what you are looking for. Can they help? Do they know anyone who may be able to help? Speak to everyone; take the ones who could be good contacts for coffee and really go through everything.

Look at joining some local networking organisations, where you meet up once a week, often over breakfast, and pitch your wares. This will get you used to talking about what you do and find you a supportive network of entrepreneurs, as it can be a bit lonely when you first start. They can also provide you with direct qualified introductions to potential customers and you will get feedback on your product offering, enabling you to tweak as you go.

I remember my first networking meeting well. Believe it or not it took me two years of selling before I discovered networking. Meeting other businesspeople and talking about your business is beneficial in so many ways. You get a chance to really develop your pitch and access to lots more customers, and I don't mean the people in the room, I mean the people they know. If you can even manage to do a presentation at a networking event it will really polish your presentation skills. Don't panic, it sounds terrible, but honestly if it were not for networking I would not have been able to do two best man speeches and many public speaking events; it is a great way to break down those barriers.

You also get to meet and share ideas with other businesspeople, see how they are dealing with problems, how they get customers, and generally see how you can collaborate for the benefit of everyone.

You are now in business properly and these are exciting times. Speak to everyone, get to know the other networkers, go with an attitude of giving, how can you help them, who can you introduce them to – Karma is alive and kicking in a networking environment. Remember you are an ambassador of your brand now, be positive, be proactive and be a useful and active member of the network.

Like anything, the more you put in, the more you will get out. Go to any event, show or seminar you are invited to, but don't sit in the corner with the one friendly face, meet people and talk to them.

I remember, about five years into my telecoms company, being invited to a networking meeting. When the day came it was a frosty winter morning, I was in bed, snug and warm when the alarm went off. Outside it was foggy and freezing, everything outside my bed was cold and my eyes were stuck together; I was shockingly tired and just needed another hour of sleep. However, I forced myself to get up, get in the shower, get in the car and drive to this golf club where the meeting was. There were only about ten people there, many others getting that extra hour I suspect. However, pretty soon I was chatting to a guy who was CEO of a large chain of wholesale warehouses. He was currently in talks with Vodafone and Orange about them selling their products through his stores. I told them we could do a similar proposition, but align ourselves more with their brand, so it was more like their offering. Within four weeks we had a pilot open in one of their stores and we went on to do around £6 million worth of business with them. Always keep an open mind, and always look for the opportunity. You never know who you will meet, and you never know what it will lead to, so get up, get in the shower and Go Do!

MILESTONE SIX – Three Months

Before you worry too much about adding a new set of achievements to your progress, take a moment to consider how far you've come. At the end of your two-month period you had defined your market and your product, put together a detailed cash flow document and registered your company. You'd taken those first tentative steps along the way to making yourself known, whether by placing your first advert, making a first set of telephone calls or by standing up and talking your business through with a potential customer or a complete stranger. You might, too, have made your first sale – or sales. You might be wondering if, in an incredibly short period of time, you've created a really promising business – your pitch gets enthusiastic responses every time – or maybe all you've garnered is polite interest when talking through your product. If so, don't panic – something needs tweaking, whether it's your price, your pitch or the product itself. These are early days, so you can do that. Remember how my businesses have changed and evolved. So long as you're adaptable and responsive to the business climate, you can keep revisiting your planning document and refining the idea. And remember never to stop learning from those around you, whether they're rival businesses, friendly mentors or learned experts whose books you continue to read to expand your knowledge.

What is the biggest achievement yet? You're in business. You've done it. Milestone six is about enjoying it and, if there are any doubts lingering, overcoming them and diving in. It's time to review your contacts database – by now you'll have a stack of business cards and phone numbers – and be ready to arrange that elusive first professional pitch with a potential customer or client. Ring around, list your targets and don't take no for an answer.

The exhilaration you'll feel when you make that sale will be fantastic. I love the fact that as an entrepreneur you can feel this excitement and exhilaration at any age. In almost all other professions you peak – sports, politics, music – and once you have peaked you will never get that feeling back. But the entrepreneur can revisit the awesome feeling of making that first sale for as long as he or she has a good idea to make a reality. Richard Branson is putting passengers into space, after all.

And you've set out on a journey of your own, too. Not into space – yet – but a few small steps towards establishing your business will prepare you for giant leaps in the future. Right now, concentrate on the customer and making those sales. When you make your first one, send a message to jeremy@jeremyharbour.com to tell me all about it. I can't tell you how pleased I'll be for you, and you should be bouncing off the walls with excitement!

You made it. You started a business and embarked upon a life-changing journey. It is time to treat yourself, in whatever way floats your boat, and then buckle down for some hard work and the ride of your life!

ABOUT THE AUTHOR

Jeremy Harbour has been runner up 'Entrepreneur of the Year' 3 times, appeared on The Money Channel, has mentored for The Prince's Trust and been involved in The Prince's Trust fundraising committee. He has also been invited to

Buckingham Palace and the House of Commons, been interviewed for *The Telegraph*, *The Sunday Times*, *The Financial Times* and many more, has written articles for *Men's Health* and *The Sharp Edge* as well as blogging. He has sponsored The Gumball Rally and founded the Harbour Club in 2009, which provides experiential training for entrepreneurs looking to learn how to acquire and sell businesses.

During a career spanning over 20 years Jeremy has started many businesses and has grown an organisation to 130+ employees with £10m+ revenues, more recently he has also completed over 30 company acquisitions, mostly distressed, and many exits. He also has great knowledge of insolvency and company law. He is renowned for being truly sector agnostic with previous business interests as diverse as a health club and spa, music school, IT support, telecoms, training, business process outsourcing, cleaning, air conditioning and a cooking school to name just a few.

Jeremy has been key note speaker at a number of events with audience sizes reaching up to 700, and has spoken in Spain, London, Singapore, Bangkok and Hong Kong. His Harbour Club groups tend to be between 5 – 10 and he provides really frank and open information including numerous case studies.

He now lives between the beautiful Balearic Island of Mallorca and South East Asia, he is a licensed boat skipper and is currently training for his private pilot's license, he has travelled extensively and is a self confessed 'deal junkie'.

WHAT PEOPLE HAVE BEEN SAYING ABOUT THE HARBOUR CLUB LIGHT

'All I can Say is "wow" with an accountancy and finance background this really hits home to see how business really works.'

Richard

'The course was brilliant, rich in experience and relevant with applied knowledge, tips and strategies,'

Dave

'Jeremy does not just think outside the box, he doesn't have a box'

Jon

'I came with high expectations and all were thoroughly exceeded'

Name withheld – senior M&A person from a division of Microsoft

'I am really pleased I followed my instinct and joined The Harbour Cub, my initial concerns have been lifted and I think this will be the start of a great adventure.'

Kam

'They say knowledge is power, well at the moment I feel very powerful! Thank you Jeremy for the opportunity.'

Rupey

'The Harbour Club course has shown me a world of possibility and a new way of thinking. The opportunities seem endless'

Grant Smee

INDEX

INDEX

INDEX

INDEX